Seven
Steeples

Seven Steeples

MARGARET HENRICHSEN

ILLUSTRATED BY WILLIAM BARSS

HOUGHTON MIFFLIN COMPANY BOSTON

The Riverside Press Cambridge

The Riverside Press
CAMBRIDGE · MASSACHUSETTS
PRINTED IN THE U.S.A.

With thanksgiving for all those whose lives
have made this book possible.

*"Not unto us, O Lord, not unto us
But unto thy name give glory."*
PSALM 115:1

AUTHOR'S NOTE

CONTRARY TO THE USUAL DISCLAIMER SAYING THAT ALL likenesses to living people are purely coincidental, in this book real people are portrayed and real names used. I have tried to paint the portraits with accuracy as well as affection. Always I have been gratefully aware of how much these people have given to me of themselves and of how fortunate I am in their friendship. In order that there may be no possible violation of that friendship everyone in the book has been given a chance to read all references to himself or his family and in each case permission has been graciously given to use the material as here presented.

If the reader misses some deeper notes that belong in a Christian ministry, may I say that there is much that is confidential between pastor and people? Many things that have come into our life together in this parish are known only to the people concerned and to the Lord in whose hand our lives are held and by whose truth our work is ultimately judged.

The spirit in which our people have accepted this story was well summed up by one woman whose permission I wanted to obtain. I read her the description, assuring her that any changes she wanted could still be made as the book was not then in print. She replied: "No I don't know as I'd change anything. The people around here all know what it was like anyhow, and the rest of the world doesn't matter."

Seven Steeples

ONE

ALL THROUGH NEW ENGLAND THERE ARE LITTLE WEED-GROWN country churchyards. I had seen them when I was on vacation. White spires are picturesque, seen against the hills, but close to, they belonged to little churches that needed paint, little churches that were not used, save for a month or two in the summer when some visiting minister held a few services, little churches that opened with painfully groaning squeaks when the neighbors went in sometimes to dust, to remove the cobwebs and prepare for an occasional funeral service for one of the older residents. I had seen day after day, the village children going by, growing up, children who had never been to church and who knew no Sunday School, children to whom the Bible stories were almost unknown, children who had no real sense of a God who loved them and to whom they were accountable and responsible. The countryside seemed to be growing godless because no minister was there who cared! If only all the ability and

devotion weren't being expended on already privileged groups!

On a particular evening in the church conference room in one of Boston's nicest suburbs there were eighteen of us gathered around a table. The director of religious education was there, very sure of herself; the minister, paternal and encouraging, the various department superintendents, some eager young teachers, the head of the men's class. I thought of my own lively group of ten-year-olds and the enthusiasm with which they had made some plans with me, and then looked at these fine able people who gave up many hours each week to their work as teachers in the church school. There were no better teachers anywhere, I felt sure. But suddenly my "dander" began to rise. It seemed so wrong for us to spend this whole evening just trying to do a good job better. These suburban youngsters had the very best of everything! The finest school system imaginable, wonderful homes for the most part, loving parents whose incomes were sufficient to provide the necessities and some of the luxuries. They were children who could look forward to college or professional training. They had a church of which to be proud—and we were proud of the job we were doing—and all of a sudden it seemed sickeningly smug! And unimportant! Any one of these eighteen people would have been such a godsend to children who didn't have all these advantages. Any one of these conscientious, well-prepared teachers might well be reaching a far greater group. All this discussion about lesson material was so trivial! These were real people, teaching real children. They could, any of them, have done a splendid piece of work regardless of the material, for they were experienced teachers and consecrated. They knew children, they had devotion, faith, and a good working knowledge of the Bible.

Chairs scraped as they were pushed back. The meeting was over, but the mood of rebellion continued. I went home to sputter a bit to my sympathetic and wise husband, who was always able to balance my impetuous feelings. "Perhaps some day you can do something about it," he comforted me. Neither of us guessed what a prophetic word it was.

It had been a year since my husband's death. Gradually out of the resulting sense of devastation, a plan for my life was forming. I had written a good friend, a former pastor in our town, to see if he thought that anywhere in the country there might be closed churches who would like to have a woman pastor, and to find out whether he thought I could be useful in such a place.

Hilda Ives had been responsible for that idea, Hilda, the great pioneer woman minister of New England. I had seen her a short while before and she had asked me what I planned to do, and then said, "Have you ever thought of the ministry?"

I had laughed at the very idea. "What would I use for money to study?" I asked. "I've got to get to work right away." (Besides, I thought, who wants a woman minister?) Aloud I said, "I haven't had a speck of theological training, you know. I couldn't qualify."

"I'm not so sure," Hilda rejoined. "Just from living and from your experience in teaching and social work you've learned some things that are not in the books, some things that students fresh from Seminary don't have yet because they haven't lived long enough. There are ways of getting the theological training as you work."

Hilda had gone but the thought lingered. The mood of that meeting in the church conference room returned, and in a few days I knew that it was the right answer for me if there should be an opening. So I had written my good friend in the northern district of Maine.

Before his answer came I had told the Children's Aid Association, which was boarding some adolescents from broken homes with me, that by June they would have to find other foster homes. I knew that I mustn't continue that sort of work, fascinating as it was. A woman alone doesn't make a home for a disturbed and disturbing youngster. It had been so different when Chris was there to be father of the family! And I had investigated the possibilities of theological training by correspondence and found that it could be managed through the Methodist Conference course of study.

One Sunday noon, in the house so horribly empty now, the telephone rang insistently as I returned from church. I dashed to answer it. A far-distant voice said, "Margaret? This is Vaughn. Will you come up to this District? I must have another pastor here right away."

I replied, "Wait a minute. I didn't ask you for a job, I just wanted your advice."

And the reply came, "Well—I asked you to come up, didn't I?" It was all the advice he ever gave.

"Give me till Tuesday night to be sure," I said. "I'll call you on Tuesday." And Tuesday night I called through to Maine and said, "I'll come." I knew one family in the state— this same preacher of the Methodist Church, now Superintendent of the Bangor District.

"Good," he said, "I think it will be Brooksville. I'm coming to Boston next week and I will see you."

When he came and showed me on the map where Brooksville was, I began to be very eager. The irregular shore-line indicated that this was seaside country, presumably beautiful and wooded. I longed for the peace and beauty to help heal the loneliness.

It was the very next morning, Wednesday, when the real estate agent, who had had our dear little house in Northampton for sale for five years without a nibble, called me to say he had a buyer for the house. I went to Northampton, cleaned out the attic, indulged in a tear or two as I relived in thought our happy years there, picked a bit of the tall-bush honeysuckle that shaded the doorway, said goodbye to the laurel bushes Chris had brought in from the woods and transplanted so lovingly, and, with a feeling that I was closing the door on a very happy period, signed the deed, paid off the mortgage, and returned to Boston with just enough money in my pocket for a second-hand car.

Two days later a car dealer called me to say he had a good buy, a used Oldsmobile that had had only one owner and had been gently treated. Poor thing—it was never again to have such gentle consideration! By the time Vaughn arrived to tell me about Brooksville I had sold the house, bought the car, and was ready to think ahead. When he heard about all this he said, "Oh, you have a car now. Well, then, I think I'll send you to Sullivan."

It was all the same to me. They were names on a map in a part of Maine I longed to see. My one hope was that I might be useful and through making a new life in new surroundings find meaning in the years that stretched so emptily ahead.

And so it was that two months from the day Hilda had first spoken to me I started for Maine, the car loaded to the roof, the two dogs in among the suitcases and boxes, the large moving van following, forty dollars in my pocket, and the future a large question mark. A capable, energetic little neighbor had agreed to drive up with me and help me settle, and her cheerful comments on the passing scene kept the time from being filled with sentimental memories or strange forebodings.

We drove through increasingly wonderful countryside. There were small villages, occasional glimpses of the sea, the shapes of pointed firs against the sky, the cry of gulls, and a growing wonder and sense of adventure in my heart. As we passed one town after another I noticed the little churches, for I was on my way to be pastor of a little church! But these were so neat, so well-painted, so prosperous-looking. Surely mine wouldn't be like this. I had pictured little run-down buildings, their doorsills sagging, their hinges rusty. These well-kept little churches must have "regular" ministers, I thought. Then suddenly I realized with sharp fear that it was up to me to be a "regular" minister. Could I measure up? I knew I couldn't. But I knew that God would work through me if I really gave Him my whole self and kept my own ego out of the way. This was His work—His grace would supply my need.

My appointment was to the Sullivan Circuit, northeast from Portland about one hundred and sixty miles. Gradually, as we drove on, the country changed. Instead of tidy lawns with shade trees and evidence of much village life, there were more and more stretches of forest land. At first, pines, spruce, and hackmatacks had been just exclamation points among the hardwoods. Now it was different, the woods were all spruce and fir and hackmatack, with only occasional maples and birches struggling to gain a foothold. Villages were farther and farther apart, more homes were unpainted, there were occasional tarpaper-covered shacks in little clearings. There was a wilder "feel." This was to be my country and already I loved it.

It was late afternoon when we arrived. Fog was coming in from the sea. I crossed the long iron bridge on Route 1 and inquired the way at the filling station. The old man there was friendly enough and told me this was Sullivan and the parsonage was about a mile up the road to the left. So many unpainted houses along this road! And then the little house that had once been white, across the way from the big brown house. This must be it. The lawn was an uncut meadow of daisies and yellow hawkweed, the little house just like so many we had passed—a straight little box with gabled ends, end onto the street. There was no porch, just a wooden doorstep that led to the green door with two narrow glass panels. I tried the door; it was locked. I looked around, half expecting some neighbor to appear with a welcoming smile—some member of the Ladies' Aid to help me move the carload of things in. Since no one was in sight I went across the street and knocked. A pleasant motherly woman came to the door. I told her I was the new minister and asked her if she knew who had the key. She replied that she didn't know much about the church affairs, they didn't go, but she thought I'd better see the Robertsons. There were several Robertson families, but "Probably Gussie has the key, I shouldn't wonder."

She told me where "Gussie" lived—up the lane behind the church. On the way to find the key I glanced at the church, frighteningly big, impressive-looking. As in so many Maine churches, the spire was at the left over the entrance. It is a type of architecture that seems to belong here and to fit right in with the pointed firs. This church had a fine

bell. The belfry was covered with shingles with rounded
ends that overlay each other like feathers, or fish scales—
appropriate for a seaside community. At the top was a
weathervane and on it a bluebird was perched, singing
joyfully. Surely a good omen.

The lane, tree-bordered, led to a very pleasant house,
with bleedingheart and delphiniums in the border and a
vine-covered porch. There Miss Robertson ushered me into
a spick-and-span kitchen, shiny with fresh varnish and
gleaming brass pipes. This was Miss Gussie's sister—but
they didn't have the key. I must have looked a bit dis-
mayed and weary, for suddenly her eyes warmed and she
said, "Can't I get you a cup of tea?"

I was famished. For some miles I had seen no sign of a
place to get dinner—lunch had been a very light, sandwich
affair. I am not very fond of tea, but I thanked her and made
conversation with the sweet-faced older woman, her mother,
while Miss Lillian bustled around and made a pot of tea.
It was strong and hot. She offered canned cream; there was
no sugar in sight. I was to learn that this was the way most
of the people had their tea, but up to that moment my idea
of tea had been a thin pale brew with a slice of lemon,
hardly more than hot lemonade. This drink had body
and substance to it. Since there was also a molasses cookie,
I managed to drink it and found it very heartening.

We returned to the subject of the key. She didn't know
where it was but thought I might try another Robertson
family, just below the parsonage. The casual way in which
nobody seemed to care whether I got in or not frightened
me. Is this the way they feel about their church? I wondered. As if it doesn't matter? Or is it because I am a
woman? There was some of both, I discovered later, espe-

cially resentment at having a woman preacher sent them by
the Conference—but mostly it was because they were shy.

The other Robertsons did have the key and Mr. Robertson actually came across the street and opened the door for
me. I saw a little narrow hall with a straight stairway that
went up almost from the doorsill, on the right a living room,
and behind it a dining room with a sideboard, an ugly
heavy table, and straight chairs. The living room had three
wicker chairs with the most elaborate curlicues I had ever
seen and a cylindrical wood-burning stove with a nickel-
embroidered petticoat around the base and a nickel "Grecian
urn" on top. I had somehow expected a fireplace, but this
stove was the heating unit for the house and almost too
effective, I was to discover when winter came. Central
heating was achieved very simply: there was a hole cut
in the ceiling, both in the dining room and in the kitchen,
to allow the heat to go upstairs. The floors were covered
with Congoleum "art-squares" which had been much washed.
The paint around the edges was of a particularly discouraged
orange-yellow. All I could think of was a squash that had
passed its usefulness. Upstairs were two large bedrooms
and a smaller one that the last pastor had used for a study.
The furniture was adequate.

Obviously someone had been in to wash the floors and
wipe down the walls. But the kitchen! I remembered my
cozy little white kitchen with its shiny modern equipment
in the home I had just left. This kitchen had a low wood-
burning range, and an iron sink, somewhat rusty, with a
big pump at the end of it. The pump didn't work. Mr.
Robertson said he guessed it needed new leathers. The
woodwork of the kitchen was the same depressing orange
color—so was the pump. But from the kitchen window was

a view of woods coming almost to the back door, and the trees were full of birds. I could stand any sort of kitchen as long as birds came to the windows!

Leading from the sink was a wooden trough which served as drain. All through those first two years I was to watch my soapsuds run down that trough whenever the dishpan was emptied, and more than once I saw the field mice use that drain as a convenient ramp for coming in. At the back of the house was a woodshed with an outhouse. At least I wouldn't have to go outdoors in stormy weather. The cellar was mostly ledge. Going down those wobbly stairs one came to the ledge, swung around it over to the back part, where one could just stand up straight between the floor joists. One corner of the cellar had been a cistern, long since cracked with the frost, a truly Biblical "empty cistern that holds no water." It had, however, perhaps two inches of stagnant water in it. Nothing like having your own home-grown mosquitoes, thought I. Lucky I wasn't subject to rheumatism. At least the two inches of water served as a cooling system in the summer, for this was right under the floor of the dining room, which was to be my study. It served me well on hot days, though I determined that someday it should be abolished. Mr. Robertson was working with the pump while I looked things over. Since the cistern wouldn't hold water there didn't seem to be much sense in trying to repair the pump. When I asked him where I could get water he suggested the pump on "Hattie's" porch. Hattie, it seemed, was my next-door neighbor to the "south'ard." She "worked away" in the summer, but everyone in the neighborhood used her well.

It was getting on toward seven o'clock. The van with all my furniture hadn't arrived, and in spite of the cup of tea I was hungry. I asked the lady across the street if she knew of anyone in town who took boarders. Well, no, she didn't. I asked her if she knew of any place where I could arrange to take my dinners out. It would give me more time to make pastoral calls and work on my sermons and study course. But my neighbor was completely discouraging about that—she didn't think there was anybody in town "who would do anything like that." There seemed nothing more to do that night but to return to Ellsworth, the county seat thirteen miles away, and stay overnight in a tourist home. So back we went, Selma and I.

Selma was used to living without conveniences. She could show me how to manage a wood fire, for my knowledge of wood fires had been limited to various camping trips. She was loyalty itself. To hear her comments on the difficulties of those first days was a cheering thing. She was so outspoken in her opinion of the situation that I found myself assuring her that it wasn't half as bad as she thought, and standing up for the congregation I had yet to meet. After all, it wasn't the congregation's fault that for some years they had had only student pastors from the Seminary in Bangor, forty miles way. The house had not been regularly lived in, only used as a sort of weekend camp for these boys.

After a good dinner, a hot bath, and a good sleep in Ellsworth, the prospect seemed less depressing. At least now I had the key! In the morning, still thick with fog, we drove back to Sullivan and found the van there waiting to unload, and with it a drove of small shy children wanting to see everything.

What would we have done without those obliging movers, who took the beds, bureaus, tables, and chairs already in the parsonage out to the garage and then began the task of bringing my furniture in? When I saw the size of the van and compared it with the house, I wondered if it wouldn't be simpler to live in the van. But almost everything went in, though how they ever got the old, high wing-backed sofa through the narrow door and around the corner into the living room is still a mystery.

The little Scotts (I learned later that there were twelve of them) who supervised the procedure had the most engaging grins I ever saw. Their soft murmurs about everything were awed comments. "Ain't that pretty?" "Artie" sat himself in an upholstered chair and remarked wonderingly, "It's soft." Then the others came to see and sit in it in their turn. The big carved-oak table and the hall chair of heavily carved oak with red leather seat, family heirlooms, simply wouldn't go in, nor were they appropriate for the simple little house. We took them over to the church. The chair looked as if it were waiting for the resident bishop. The big table was placed in the vestibule of the church for a while; now it is being used by a neighbor. My oriental rugs were warm-looking as they lay on top of the art squares, though the three-toned effect was somewhat surprising— the rugs, the patterned Congoleum, and the sad orange border around the floor. Sometime I may paint the floor again, but it helps me to remember what it could be like, and what it was like for my predecessors!

With my own furniture, pictures, rugs, and books, things began to look more homelike. Instead of the curlicued wicker chairs there was the mahogany drop-leaf table between the front windows, with Mother's silver candlesticks on it, and the old Sheffield fruit dish. Grandfather's old bookcase filled the study corner, with the Indian pottery on top of it which Father had brought back from the far

West when we were children. The old wing-backed sofa, on which we had recuperated from chicken pox, measles, and other childhood ailments, still had the power to make me feel safe and comfortable. The shabby chair which the Boy Scouts had given us for a wedding present, and the shabbier one which had belonged to a favorite uncle—all seemed to fit in as if they belonged. Monday, the day of arrival, had been the anniversary of my husband's birthday. It gave me a little warm feeling that he was sharing this new adventure with me and approved. I still missed him dreadfully, but he seemed close, for he too had loved wilderness country and had a marvelous understanding and appreciation of people. He would have taken to these people, and they to him. I hoped I could learn to love them as genuinely and unselfishly as he would have.

Two of my pictures, paintings that told of happy vacations we had had together in New Hampshire, were too large for the parsonage. So we took them to the church and hung them on the front wall on either side of the pulpit. They were surely more inspiring to look at than dirty varnish, and since they were mountain scenes they seemed appropriate as a spot to which one could lift the eyes.

The church was dark inside, but had an air of real dignity. The hangings were maroon, the pews varnished wood, the pulpit and chairs of good line. To my utter amazement, the door proved to be at the front of the church instead of at the back. Everyone came in right beside the pulpit platform and had to go down the side aisle to get to the back pews, which everyone did! I have sometimes wondered if an extension were built on churches, whether people would still head for the farthest possible corner? Is it a fear of being too closely under the parson's eye, or a false modesty that thinks it more humble to sit at the back? Anyhow, there is a forest of empty pews to preach across before one reaches the congregation.

The windows of the church were frosted glass on the lower half, colored squares in the upper. Little squares of red and blue and yellow and purple floated across the quiet, strangely dignified building. How the children must love to watch the mysterious bits of color, I thought, remembering my own childhood and what fun it was to look out through such windows and see the world all green or fiery red or bright blue. I sat in the second pew from the front and bowed my head and waited in stillness for some time, just asking God to make me a real minister of Jesus Christ to these people.

Thursday the fog lifted. I saw the sun for the first time in Maine, and to my joy saw that I had a fine view of a mountain from my front windows. They told me it was "Schoodic." This was confusing, for I knew that some distance down the coast was a point of land known as Schoodic. Later on I made a new friend who lived thirty-five miles away and had a Schoodic lake in her neighborhood. But I found that Schoodic is Indian for burnt-over land. No wonder the name appeared so frequently. For centuries forest fires have taken their sad toll.

The walk to the post office each day proved fascinating. There were two nice stretches of woods to pass, with birds singing everywhere. I heard hermit thrushes and veerys and olive-backed thrushes in there every morning. Oven-birds and red-eyed vireos sang constantly. Children along the way stared curiously at me, but the two dogs, Pinny and Woozle, were always a good introduction, and since Pinny,

the red cocker, and the Woozle beast, a friendly old fellow
of shepherd-collie ancestry, were devoted to children, it
didn't take long to get acquainted. Whenever I asked any
of the children, "How are you today?" the answer would
come back, "Go-od." How they contrive to make it sound
like a two-syllable word I don't know, but they do. And
that one word is sufficient answer to any questions about
health. Along with their soft voices, these children have an
instinctive unstudied courtesy that was refreshing after the
difficult, disturbing and disturbed youngsters with whom I
had been dealing.

The dogs thought this a wonderful place—woods and
fields everywhere, with squirrels to be chased, porcupines
to puzzle them, and skunks to be avoided. On that first
morning walk to the post office they dashed gaily ahead,
exploring everything. We had passed the second stretch of
woods, when with a sudden burst of excitement both dogs
went tearing around a house that sat back from the road
under a majestic pine. Right up on the back porch went
Woozle, while two startled cats leaped spitting to the railing
and three others disappeared under the house. A lady, hearing the tumult, appeared on the back porch with a broom
in her hand. Oh dear, I thought, a fine start, this, in human
relations! I went up to apologize but was met in the friend-
liest manner possible as she said, "That don't matter. It's
the nature of dogs to chase cats. You must be the minister!"
Somehow her smile and her comprehension of dogs as well
as of her beloved cats took me into her heart. It was the
first real welcome I had felt.

Her husband was the postmaster, and at the little post
office across the street I got acquainted with the white-
haired gentleman who was known affectionately as "Siddie"

to young and old. It was a shock to my schoolteacherish notions of children's bringing-up to hear a little seven-year-old say to him, "Any mail for us, Siddie?"

Without thinking I exclaimed, "Don't you think you ought to say 'Mr. Havey'?"

Orchis looked at me in amazement. She had clearly never heard of such an idea. It marked me as a "foreigner" for sure! It was my first much-needed lesson in waiting to see how things were before speaking out.

It wasn't long before I was calling him Siddie, too. And I am perfectly sure that the little back room at the post office, where men of all ages congregated before mail time, has had more helpful conversations in it, and a stronger influence for good, than anything the church has been able to do here for years.

By this time I was used to getting my water from the well next door—enjoying the view of Schoodic on one side and Cadillac Mountain on the other as I pumped my pails full. I certainly see the need for the shoulder yokes that women of Holland wear to balance their pails and leave their hands free for other things. Two pails full in the morning, another two at noon, and another two at night carried me through, except when I had a washing to do. The water was good but the pump was rusty, and if the water stood in the pails overnight there was a bright orange film of rust across it the next morning which made it unfit to drink. (Too bad, I thought, that one can't absorb iron into the blood this way. How full of energy I might have been!) The pail soon got a permanent orange tinge—I wondered if my interior was similarly colored!

To haul and heat water enough for a good bath was quite a job, especially for one who had been used to plumbing all her life. The old tin tub on the kitchen floor was picturesque but somehow didn't bring much relaxation. Bathing became a stern duty, not a luxurious joy. But by autumn I had got well enough acquainted with a neighbor to discover that she had a good water supply and a bathroom but no washing machine. My washing machine, our first big investment after we were married, was standing idle in the shed. It seemed as if something more intelligent and more Christian could be worked out. So one day, while we were talking and I was thinking what hard work it must be for her to keep her family clean, I asked her if she would consider housing my washing machine and having the use of it in exchange for weekly baths. It proved to be a first-rate plan. Every other Monday I would take over my washing and do it there in my own machine while she used the machine all she wished between times. And then on Saturday afternoons I would go down to her house, have a real tub bath, and stay for a supper of the most delicious baked beans and hot rolls I have ever eaten.

They tasted so good after my sketchy cooking, for it was hard for a tall person to cook on that little low range. The grates were warped and the oven wouldn't bake evenly. And I, used to gas stoves all my life, found a fire on hot days quite unbearable. My electric coffee percolator helped a lot. I could get a quart of boiling water in a few minutes and by adding enough cold to make it usable I had enough for dishes for an ordinary meal. I got small amounts for washing out personal things the same way, and found it was perfectly possible to boil an egg or a potato, or cook peas in the percolator. I could avoid having a fire on the hottest days.

And that was good, for there was very little wood in the

shed. I asked Siddie and Miss Robertson and others about getting wood. Always the answer was the same: "I don't know where you'll get any." This was during the war, few people were cuting firewood, though it grew all around us. The government was paying well for pulp and paper and anybody who worked in the woods was cutting soft wood for pulp. One neighbor assured me that I would have to "hook on to an oil stove." By August I did manage to find a man who had some good wood and ordered six cords of hardwood, but when it came the first load was half cedar—no good for cooking or kindling either.

Down the road was a charming house. Shingled, vine-covered, it sat lower than most. Actually, it was built right on the ground with no foundation under it, I learned when it was taken down some years later. A little old lady lived there alone. After I had been here perhaps five weeks I met her on the street. I said, "Good morning—how are you?" and I got the usual "Go-od," spoken in the lovely soft voice which is such a rest after city voices.

Then she peered up at me anxiously and said, "Do you like it here?"

"I love it," I said. "I think I like it better than any place I've ever lived." Her face broke into a wonderful smile like the sun coming out, and I was thrilled. It was the first sign I'd seen that anyone was glad I liked the town. Up to then I had felt, perhaps wrongly, that they were simply tolerating me until the District Superintendent could come to their rescue with a man.

Later, when the neighbor whose cats had been dispersed so unceremoniously that first morning said to me, "I don't care for you," I thought, Well, that's probably the way most of them feel. I've always heard Maine people were frank. What do I say to that? Not knowing what to say, I kept still. She repeated it. "I don't care for you at all." And then "No, I don't care for you no more than as if you was my sister!" It was the most wonderful compliment I had ever had. Something lonely in my heart let go and I began to feel that truly this was where I was meant to be.

TWO

"LET US SING HYMN ONE HUNDRED AND THIRTY-FIVE," I SAID.
There was a slight stir at the back of the church. I looked
up to see a tall gaunt woman on crutches coming in through
the door. Neat and forthright, she swung herself capably
into a pew near the back. I made a mental note of the
crutches, determined to find out who she was and where
she lived. Surely this would be a good place to begin the
pastoral calling the next day. This was the "other church"
of the circuit, a tidy little church in a neat fishing village.
It was a charming village, with its gray and white houses
set along the water's edge, their lobster pots piled up beside
them, the little harbor peaceful with its boats riding at anchor, the dark red buildings of the sardine factory at the
curve of the shore, and the purposeful flight of the gulls
as they flew ceaselessly overhead, curving their strong
wings to catch the air currents, ceaselessly crying.

This church was as cheerful as the other one was somber.

The congregation, with a good percentage of men in it, I noticed gratefully, sang as if they liked to go to church. How their voices rang out on the old hymns. Happy at their responsiveness, I continued with the Scripture and entered into the pastoral prayer. I had hardly spoken three sentences when a deep "Amen" came forth from someone. It was wonderful to feel the enthusiasm of this group, for the Scotch restraint in North Sullivan had been hard to preach against. There I could see scarcely a flicker of facial expression, but here there were smiles, nods, amens—a sense that they were with me all the way. What an alive church it was!

The next day I drove down again to begin my pastoral calling. The roads were embroidered with daisies. They were lovely under the soft feathery green of the hackmatacks. I found the house of the lady with the crutches, an immaculate gray house with a large flagpole in front. In fact I didn't have to inquire, for as I came along the road she was coming up from the spring with a pail of water in each hand, the crutch tucked up under her arm. I ran to take the pails from her and walked along to the house. She invited me into the most gleaming kitchen I had ever seen. I made note of the shining black of her sink. I must learn from her what to do about the rust in mine, I thought. The end of her pump was covered with a piece of wax paper held on with a rubber band. No wandering fly was going to have a chance to cross that pump spout. She invited me to sit down, and when I chose the straight chair, urged me to take the rocker. I asked her how she had hurt her leg.

"I was taking a pie to the supper put on by the Sisterhood, and I was just stiverin' along mindin' my own business," she answered. "No reason for it at all. Makes me mad. I've done a man's work in the woods many a time since the

Cap'n died. Shingled my own shed roof last summer—and I'm past seventy. Never had a mite of trouble. Then goin' along to this supper I had to fall. And didn't it pain? Didn't hurt the pie, though—not a mite. Crust didn't even get cracked!"

I expressed my sympathy. We talked along about other things. Guardedly she gave me bits of information about the village and the church. She didn't think much of the tendency of modern times to treat Sunday "just as if 'twas a day like any other. I wasn't brought up that way—no sir!" She gave an emphatic nod of her strong head. "Why last week a horse fell through my well curb. 'Twas a job to get him out—broke the well curb all to bits. Do you think I could get a man to mend that curb? No sir! Wouldn't nobody do it less they did it on Sunday. I wouldn't hear to it. Never did have any work done on Sunday, I don't aim to begin now."

"Is it still broken?" I asked, wondering about her own safety as she went out there through the long grass with her crutch.

"Oh no. I got some boards and my saw and hammer and fixed it myself. 'Twant easy with my leg in a cast—but I saw no good ever come of work done on Sunday. The Lord gave us other days to get our work done."

"Aunt Ada" and I grew to be the closest sort of friends. Often after church I'd drop in to get her salty common sense and deeply devoted spirit, which were like a tonic. She confided to me once that she had had a daughter who would have been just my age if she had lived. "She'd have looked like you some, too," she added wistfully. I could well believe it. Aunt Ada was nearly six feet tall, her bones were big, her frame strong, her features vigorous. I am built on

large proportions too. I felt all the closer as I saw her whisk
a tear out of her eye. "The cat's foot!" she exclaimed. "I'm
a foolish old woman. Here, can't you use some of my
pickle?" She opened the cupboard door and dusted off a
jar as she gave it to me, though how there could have been
a speck of dust in the cupboard I don't see. On the inside
of the open door I noticed a row of measuring spoons, a
can opener, a small tea strainer and other little kitchen
gadgets, all shining, and each one on its own hook, from
which there hung also a small lace-paper doily to protect the
paint from the rubbing of the utensil. Such dainty house-
keeping for this strong-minded soul who could cut wood
better than most men, would "hire out" to paper other people's houses—as everybody said, "she was a lovely hand to
paper"—and who chose to shingle her own roof at seventy.

She was a fine source of information about the local scene.
"Why do they call it Wonsqueak?" I asked her, referring to
a tiny settlement a short distance away.

Her eyes twinkled as she replied. "Well, they tell about
an Indian chief that wanted a certain squaw. She wouldn't
have him so he chased her right out to the edge of the cliff
and when she saw she couldn't get away she jumped off
and fetched up with just one squeak."

Once she confided to me, after we had known each other
for a while, "I knowed you was all right the first time I saw
you in church, when I see you fold your hands and close
your eyes. I don't take no stock in anybody has to read his
prayers." I gave thanks that the dear Lord had kept me
from that procedure on my first evening with them.

Many a meal I had in that house, though Aunt Ada would
never hear to my pleading that we eat in the kitchen, where
I knew she took her meals when she was alone. The sunny,
cheerful room with its spotless oilcloth-covered table was

where we always sat to talk, except on Sunday nights. Then we sat in the parlor. But when I came for a meal we had to go into the dining room. After all, I was the minister and it was fitting that the minister should be served in the dining room! So out would come her lace tablecloth and her good dishes and I would sit and look at an oil painting of two dead ducks while she plied me with delicious food invariably served with the remark, "If you can eat any of this mess."

And sometimes after supper, when the talk had gone to the deeper places of our thinking, we would kneel together by her rocking chair in a prayer for God's guidance and direction in our lives. Always she thanked God "for this dear sister" in a loud clear voice that might surely have found Heaven's ear if her humble, sincere heart had not already done so. I was a better person for those times of prayer together.

One night, several years later, she wasn't in church. My heart sank, for I knew something serious must have happened. If Aunt Ada was in town on Sunday evening she was in church, and I knew she was in town, though of late years she had spent the winters with her nephew near Portland. She always dreaded going—would declare she wouldn't go, would talk much about how lonesome she was there, yet she went, for she knew it was the sensible thing to do. The one bright spot in her winter was Skippy, the nephew's dog. Aunt Ada didn't like dogs, as she loudly declared, but Skippy was her shadow, slept on her bed, was given the choicest pieces of meat which the family never even saw, and was the subject of her conversation all summer. She could hardly wait to get back to Skippy, all the while declaring that she had no use for dogs!

That night when her place in the church was empty I

had to take another member of the church family home—
she lived some ten miles away. But then I returned; I knew
Aunt Ada would be expecting me to look her up. I found
the house brightly lighted. In her neat black silk, she was
sitting in her rocking chair in the front room. She rose to
greet me and I saw at once that something was terribly
wrong. She didn't look like herself, her face was drawn, her
passage across the room was unsteady and sidling. I thought
she had had a shock.

She told me that she had felt terribly on Thursday. "I
thought you'd be having my coat, sure enough." She had
told me the winter before that if anything happened to her
I was to have her winter coat, which was new and very
good. It was a bit too small for me but that hadn't entered
into her thought, she was so eager for me to have it. "I
thought you'd be having my coat sure, but then I felt better.
Started for Sabbath school this morning but something happened on the way. I don't know what but I couldn't make
it. Thought I'd best come back and be quiet."

"Have you had the doctor?"

"The cat's foot! No. 'Course I ain't. I'll be all right. Can't
kill an old fool like this critter."

"Well, would you let me go for him?"

"No I won't, and there's no use to ask me."

"Now look, Aunt Ada," I said. "It just doesn't make sense
for you to feel like this and not get some help. I've got to
go over to the doctor's myself tonight for a checkup. (I went
periodically, so it might as well be now.) How about your
going with me?"

"Well, I might do that—if you're sure you was going anyhow—"

So we started out. The doctor examined her thoroughly.

Then as she came out to the waiting room I went in. "How about it?" I asked him. He shook his head.

"I don't know why she's here now, with a heart like that," he said. "I've told her she's got to go right to bed and stay there."

Together we went back to the waiting room. "Who can you get to stay with you for a few days?" the doctor asked. "You've got to be absolutely quiet for a week or ten days."

"I think my sister-in-law will come," she said. I knew the sister-in-law who lived in a village not far away.

"Why don't you let me take you home and get you into bed," I suggested. "Then I'll go over and get your sister-in-law tonight and you won't have to think anything more about it." I simply couldn't leave her alone that night, I thought. Besides, whom could she send in the morning? She had no telephone.

She turned to the doctor. "Couldn't I ride with her over to Winter Harbor?" she asked. Did she fear to be left alone?

"Yes," said the doctor. "That won't hurt you any more than sitting still in your own house. But you mustn't get out of the car."

So we started for Winter Harbor. The road was dark and the night was cold, but her hand clutching mine was burning. My finger slid along her pulse. It was a running thread.

"We'll be there soon," I said. But presently she cried out, "My head, my head—oh—such a headache!" I stopped the car for a moment and held her. I could feel her quivering. Then she said, "No, we must hurry to get Grace." So on we went.

As we turned the corner of the village she managed to tell me where the house was; she had slumped in her seat against my shoulder. I drew up to the house—completely dark—and said, "I'll get Grace and we'll be right back. Just hang on." I pounded frantically at the door. Finally a window opened overhead and Grace put her head out. When I explained she said she would be right down. In a moment the door opened. I told her quietly how sick Aunt Ada appeared to be and said, "I'll go back to her while you dress." I got back to the car. Aunt Ada slid over and laid her head on my shoulder, her breath coming in short quick gasps. As Grace arrived at the car she gave a last faint sigh and moved into the heaven in which she had such confident faith. And somehow I am sure that if she could have chosen she would have wanted it just that way. No long hard illness, no helplessness, just stepping out of my car into the Light.

From the back seat, Grace held her away from my shoulder while I drove back to the doctor's. After he had made his pronouncement he went with us to a fisherman's house and then we drove back to her home, where the two men carried her in and laid her on the mattress I had hastily dragged down from upstairs. Back to the doctor's to telephone the nephew in Portland and get his instructions— then back to wait until the undertaker could get there. It was two in the morning when I finally got home.

Two days later we had a simple service in the church that she loved. But still I often look up from the pulpit toward the door to remember a tall figure as I saw her that first night, on crutches, the mannish felt hat pulled down on her head, the clear, honest discrimination between the real and sham in her thinking, and the love in her heart for the Cap'n whom she had gone to join, for Skippy, and for the pastor who looked as her daughter might have looked.

Down the road where the view was loveliest of all, with

the dark islands and points bordering the shining bay, and the daisies, buttercups, hawkweed and Indian paintbrush making a riotous carpet of color, stood a little unpainted house in the middle of a field. In spite of the surrounding beauty, there were no trees near the house to soften its uncompromising lines. They told me Pauline lived there, a girl who had been sickly for years—rheumatic fever, they said. I went to call. The upstairs of the house was not finished: Pauline's room was partitioned off from the rest of the attic by wallboard. It was papered with brown wrapping paper put on smoothly with large roofing buttons. They made a pattern of squares, up and down and across. Mosquito netting was tacked across the open window but the day was hot and only the faintest breeze managed to get through into the stifling room. Pauline's large, dark beautiful eyes stared up at me, her mouth, so little and pinched, managed to say "Hello."

In that bare hot room that day there was not one beautiful thing to look at, though when I visited again there was a spray of delphinium in a milk bottle, bravely defying the barrenness of the brown wrapping paper. But outside was breathtaking beauty of mountains and islands rising out of a sparkling sea. Pauline couldn't see it. She was lying flat— the light hurt her eyes. My heart ached. Here was a girl in her twenties, who should have been at her happiest and best, lying helpless day after day. Her mother, a large kindly woman, was obviously worried and discouraged. Life was hard for the whole family. The son was in Germany, the other daughter away from home most of the time. She loved Pauline, but there was so little that anyone could do. Although she had had one doctor after another, nobody had been able to give more than temporary help. The child, for she seemed very young in spite of her years, made mono-syllabic replies to my efforts at conversation, and smiled faintly once or twice, but the mother sat in the doorway and took over most of the conversation.

After a while I got up to go, answered Pauline's shy "Will you come again?" with a hearty assurance that I would, and picked my way out through the shed, trying not to step on two or three cats who were underfoot, making my way by a barking dog and realizing that the clutter of tin cans, papers, empty boxes, bottles, and old potato sacks was bound to accumulate in a house where there was no truck and no energetic young man to take things to the dump. My own would have been in the same state (minus the cats), were it not for a kindly neighbor.

Only a mile or two farther on I turned in at another gate. Still vividly aware of that hot, bare little room, I hardly noticed the sign, "Tranquillity Farm." I drove through a long avenue of enormous old spruce trees to find one of the loveliest places I have ever seen, big white house with wide wide porches, beautiful lawns, a cutting garden full of bright blossoms, trimmed hedges, a rose garden with a sundial in the center, and a wonderful view of sea with the mountains beyond. A pleasant-faced Scotch maid in uniform ushered me into the large living room with its beautiful rugs. Hepple-white furniture, old engravings, and damask rose-covered sofa and chairs. A needlepoint screen stood by the fireplace. On the mantel were Dresden figurines and everywhere vases of flowers, beautiful flowers beautifully arranged. This was the summer home of William Jay Schieffelin, whose family had been coming here for years. It was on this point that some of our people worked, but the contrast between this splendid room and the little house from which I had just come was almost more than I could stand.

Presently Mrs. Schieffelin came in, one of the most gracious and most sincerely devout people I have ever known. She was warm and friendly and genuine. I felt that she was taking my measure—her searching eyes probed mine, but she put me at ease immediately. How much she knew about the lives of the village people! No wonder. Not only had she watched many of them grow up, but she had always kept track of them. Each summer she would call on every family in the village. She wore charming and elaborate flowered hats, and dressed for the afternoon, with her pearls and her white gloves, she would drive up to our little houses, pick her way through the dooryards and sheds, and visit with such friendliness that the townspeople felt no hint of patronage—only the most genuine delight. Helen Preble, grandmother of twelve, and Mrs. Schieffelin, grandmother of some sixteen and great-grandmother to many more, met on common ground as they compared notes about babies' formulas and daughters' difficulties, and each of them truly appreciated the worth of the other.

Every week this outstanding family attended church in the little Ashville chapel which they had helped to build. They filled the front pews with their children, grandchildren, and some enchanting brown-eyed great-grands between two and seven years old. With their guests and the members of the household staff who attended with them, the little church was almost filled during July and August. Here the village people who worked on their place were the hosts and hostesses, but all distinctions between permanent residents and "summer people," between employers and employees, were dropped and together all were one—worshipers of God. This combination of different interests and different backgrounds united for the Kingdom of God in the little chapel seemed a demonstration of what all the world might

be. It seemed almost a microcosm of the Kingdom of God
on earth. Not that the people who made up the congregation were saints, not any of them, but there was an atmosphere of love which made it a beautiful church in spite
of the embossed metal walls, gray with the grime of years,
the sunburned and flyspecked copy of the Ten Commandments which hung from the back wall, and the folding chairs
which creaked and groaned continually as an undertone to
the service. We were to see that beauty of inner spirit given
outward expression before many years, and the little chapel
become a demonstration of how truly beautiful a one-room
church can be when simplicity, good taste, love, and generosity are combined.

One evening, the supper dishes done, I was settling down
to read, when there came a knock at the door. In the gathering dusk I saw a man whose name I did not know but whom
I had seen in the store and the post office—a tall man with a
pleasant weather-seamed face. He stood, his blue striped
painter's cap in hand, asking, "You're the minister?"

"Yes," I said. "Won't you come in?"

He came in shyly, sat down on my big sofa, and shifted
his hat to his other hand. He seemed completely over-
whelmed and found it hard to state his errand. "What can I
do for you?" I asked.

"I want to get married," he answered.

"Oh tell me about it." I thought of course he was wanting
to make plans for the future. His shirt, clean but unironed,
and the work cap hardly suggested right then and there,
but his answer was, "She's in the car."

When "she" came in I recognized her as the mother of
three children whose father's funeral I had held a few weeks

before. Notified of the death one morning, I had gone out
to the little house, to find three bewildered teen-age children. An older brother was in the service, but these three
were doing the best they could, the older girl cooking and
keeping house for her father and her younger sister and
brother. The mother, I had been told, had left some years
before and was living away from home. She had come to
the funeral, however, and I had wondered about her. Now,
here she was, looking pale and weary, for, explained the
groom, "She's just come out of the hospital."

We talked together a few minutes, and when I remarked
that unselfishness was the keynote for married happiness
they seemed to make some response. It was my first wedding.
I hoped they didn't guess. My license from the state had
arrived only the week before and I had often wondered what
I would say if I had been asked to officiate before it came.
Now it was safely here in a box on the hall chest, proclaim-
ing to all that I had the authority of the State of Maine to
perform this service. I had a deep longing, as I looked at
their worn faces, to have the occasion beautiful for them.
There were no flowers in the house, but I cleared the drop-
leaf mahogany table of its magazines and books, lighted
the tall white candles in their silver holders, propped my
open Bible against Mother's Sheffield fruit dish, and went
out in the hall to put on my robe. That this wedding should
have sacred significance for these people, I resolved to give
it all the dignity and beauty I could. With my silver cross
about my neck and the service book in my hand, I confronted
them, then realized that they had no witnesses.

Whom could we get? I named the neighbors who might
be available. Their eyes sparked to one name. So we waited
while the groom went down the street to get these people,

who had already prepared for bed and had to be persuaded to get dressed again and come. This gave me a chance for a bit of further conversation with the bride before the groom returned. Then we went forward with the service but, as I proceeded, with a prayer in my heart that their lives would have a real awareness of God and that His blessing would be with them, I was engulfed by a feeling of responsibility, and in my confusion lost my place in the service book. The ring had been put on the bride's finger as the groom haltingly followed me through those words, so solemn and meaningful. Where was I? My eye scanned the page and in a second I found myself reading the final prayer of blessing. Only as they went out the door did I realize that I had completely left out one paragraph of the service, the words which pronounced them "husband and wife together"! Perhaps they didn't notice the omission. I am sure that the Lord God, who knew the depths of their lives through the past years, and the bride's weariness and weakness, and the husband's desire to take care of her, knew that they were husband and wife in the truest sense, whether I had said so or not.

Out of curiosity I checked later with a prominent lawyer, who assured me that since the vows had been taken they were indeed legally married. I felt relieved. They have moved back into town now, their little house under the big maple is gay with geraniums in the window boxes, and their contented expressions as they pass me in the street make me feel that all is well.

THREE

THE GOLD AND GREEN OF SUMMER HAD GRADUALLY GIVEN WAY to a world all gold and russet and mauve. Against the glory of yellow birches, flaming maples and elms that dripped russet, the spruces seemed almost black. The spidery hackmatacks which had been masquerading as evergreens all summer began to show their true nature, just a soft lightness among the evergreens, almost no color at all when the other yellow and orange shades were at their height, later to be a burnt-out gold when other leaves had dropped. Across the uplands the ground carpet was a paisley of every shade of glowing red, from deepest purply crimson to bright orange. Blueberry carpets are surely the loveliest gound cover in the world. In the distance they made the mountains red-purple like moorlands covered with heather. Every trip down the road was an experience of worship and it was hard to stick to one's desk when each swirling leaf changed the pattern,

and white-throated sparrows and thrushes sang and chirped as they prepared for their southward trip. But fall meant settling down to work. The first summer had been a time of getting acquainted. With the increasing "zip" in the air there was an increasing desire to begin to build, and with so much to be done it was hard to know where to start.

Early in September we were summoned to "Pastors' Training School" at one of the lovely Maine lakes in the center of the state. The grounds were those of the Y.M.C.A. camp, now closed for the season, whose facilities were rented to the Conference before the camp was dismantled. The District Superintendent asked me if I would drive a neighboring minister—the nearest Methodist "preacher family," who lived thirty-five miles farther "Down East." I arranged to meet my passenger in Ellsworth, and found a woman about my own age. She was tall, not handsome but pleasant-looking, with a mass of beautiful reddish hair, a lovely voice, and, as I was soon to discover, a fellow interest in birds and a great love of poetry. She is one of the most spiritually sensitive people I have ever known. We were to become fast friends, but on that first morning as I drove with Erma beside me I wondered about this first meeting with the other pastors of the state.

I need not have worried. They were both brotherly and friendly. The older men who were the instructors were busy, courteous, but not especially aware that I was a newcomer who didn't know the ropes. The younger men, many of them with young wives, were a very congenial group. And there were other women pastors. We were housed together in a cabin with double-decker bunks. There was Alice, beautifully groomed and well poised, who obviously didn't feel well and spent much of her time between classes resting.

They told me her husband was a Chaplain with an overseas unit. There was Lola, a pastor of long experience. With her was Evelyn, a young and pretty farmer's wife, who was preaching in the little church in her own town. She and Lola worked together, for their parishes adjoined. There was Kathleen, small, quiet, but full of fun. Her black eyes would snap as she joined in pleasant repartee with the young men, who obviously found the rest of us a group apart.

The week was full of interest and it was good to be studying again, getting some direction by which to focus one's reading. There was much to be learned: Bible Study, Psychology of Religion, Church History, Pastoral Counseling. The study course which was to be a major concern for the next five years was carefully outlined in a study guide. There were papers to write on almost every chapter of every book and there were twelve books a year, six of them requiring examinations as well as the many papers to be written. The week-long Pastors' School was a co-ordinating and review period for books already read, with examinations on the final day. In addition to our study classes there were two special lectures each day, besides the devotional hour.

How I loved the feeling of being part of a larger group. Up to that point I had been working alone. Here was a wonderful assemblage of people, each in his own assigned place doing what I was trying to do in my parish. How eagerly I listened to the table conversation to find out how others were meeting their problems, and how reassuring to find that our problems were similar. There was time for swimming, for early morning bird rambles with Erma, and for fun. On stunt night the women came up with a song-and-dance number to the tune of "O Susanna!" with this inspired lyric:

Oh we are women ministers of good old Pine Tree State,
We work up in the country, that's a woman parson's fate,
We milk the cows, we hoe the spuds, we even chop the wood,
And then we preach on Sunday, boy, we think we're pretty good!

The minister's a busy man as you will all agree,
Just add a piled-up laundry and a missionary tea,
The telephone is ringing, there's a wedding at the door,
And the District Superintendent is expected just at four.
Brothers, Brothers, we lead a busy life,
We choose to be the minister and have to be her wife!

But underlying the fun and the study, there was always the deep sense of call. With all their individual gifts and abilities, personal characteristics and quirks, these people counted not at all as individuals but rather in their common wish to be instruments in the hands of God—to be witnesses to One whose claim on their lives was not to be denied. As Dr. Hickman concluded his final address, I slipped away from the others, to be alone for a moment under the stars that shone so clearly through the dark treetops. I could hear the laughter and chatter behind me but it was immaterial; something very deep was stirring inside my being. I felt an in-filling Presence. No matter what later experience might come, this was in itself a moment of personal ordination. I knew what the Apostle Paul meant when he talked about "The Spirit itself bearing witness with our spirit that we are the children of God."

About ten miles from the parsonage was the town of Franklin. There was a Methodist church there—a fine building sadly in need of paint—which had been closed for twelve

years. The District Superintendent had said when he assigned me to "Sullivan and Prospect Harbor," "See what
you can do with Franklin!" So now that fall was settling in
I set out to see what the situation was. It didn't take long.
I had been given the name of a fine young woman, the
local telephone operator. I went to see her in her lovely old
house, so cool and comfortable with its wide paneling, open
fireplaces, and general air of perfect order. Mrs. Blaisdell
was as trim as her house—with her softly waved hair and
her crisp house dress of cool gray matching her gray eyes.
Very politely and gently she told me that she would love to
see the old church opened, they all would, but it couldn't
be done and she advised against trying to do it. It seems
that water had got into the basement and frozen and that
the concrete foundations for the wood-burning furnace were
cracked and damaged so that the heating was out of line
and would have to be rebuilt. "Besides I don't know where
you'd find any wood." I had heard that story before! The
organ was old and wheezy, out of repair, and even if it were
fixed nobody knew how to play it. And moreover the old
people who had a real love for the church were mostly gone,
or at least so feeble they couldn't take any responsibility,
and the younger people were all established in the Baptist
church—"those that would go anywhere." I gathered that
Mrs. Blaisdell and a few others in town were staunch Epis-
copalians, and although they would support the local church
their real sense of belonging was to the Episcopal diocese.
A rector came over once a month from Mount Desert Island
and held Communion services in one of the homes. She was
friendly and sincere and I felt that with her knowledge of
the town her advice was good. She ended by saying she

wouldn't want me just to take her word for it, and suggested that I go to see "Aunt Minnie" Hardison—one of the old members whose love for the church had held firm through the years.

Aunt Minnie lived in an old farmhouse on top of a hill, with a wonderful view of Schoodic Mountain across the pasture—and "hog bay," the narrow terminus of the salt water of Frenchman's Bay that curved around behind my parsonage in Sullivan, stretched out below across a bit of blueberry land. The whine of a sawmill on the shore of the bay sounded in my ears as I entered the long low screened porch and stopped short in surprise in the kitchen. For there over the doors and the mantelpiece was a veritable arsenal of ancient guns, muskets, pistols, and knives—pieces from the Civil and Spanish Wars. Aunt Minnie had snow-white hair, appleblossom skin, and keen blue eyes, and greeted me pleasantly but with a good deal of reserve. She was a dressmaker and her huge worktable-desk was covered with neatly folded pieces of work. Uncle John, who had built the desk for her with his own hands, was out around the barn. I had seen him as I entered—a spare old man with an easy, friendly manner and a remarkable "know-how" about herbs. He gathered and dried them as his mother had before him. Bunches of tansy, pennyroyal, and thoroughwort hung from the barn rafters; strings of dried apple rings were hanging behind the stove, and the sweet smell of hay came in through the windows.

"Aunt Minnie" she was to everybody for miles around, though to me at this meeting, Mrs. Hardison. I noticed her scrutiny of my dress. Finally, with great directness she said, "Do you mind if I tell you your dress is much too short?"

"Of course I don't mind," I said. I had come from the city

where clothes were being worn short. Moreover, it was war time and it was almost impossible to get anything in the larger sizes. But obviously Aunt Minnie thought it improperly short for a minister. "What would you do?" I asked. "They just aren't making things my size."

It was plain enough what she thought I ought to do, but she was too polite to say it. She thought I ought to make my own clothes and have them right! But her keen eyes softened as I appealed to her for advice and she said, "Well, it is a problem to get anything to wear these days. Maybe I could let it down for you—if there's anything to let down." She examined the hem, decided there wasn't much, and closed her lips firmly over her opinion of modern ready-made clothes.

It was one of those hot September days—not yet Indian summer, for there had not been much frost except in the low places. Hardly a breath of air stirred even there on "Hardison's Hill" where there was "most always a breeze." As we sat and talked, my eye wandered to the most remarkable old picture I had ever seen. One of the earlier colored prints, it showed an Arctic scene with Eskimos and fur-clad sealers perched on sheer icebergs. Just to look steadily at it for a few minutes lowered my temperature so that I actually shivered. "What a wonderful picture for a day like this!" I remarked. Aunt Minnie nodded.

She agreed with the telephone operator that there wasn't anything that could be done about opening the church now. Before I left she offered me a glass of cold milk and a molasses cookie, and when I was ready to go, protested with "You don't have to hurry!" I was to learn that this was the standard phrase for a departing guest and, whether the visit had been a "dooryard call" of ten minutes or an all-day visitation, a guest was always told at the end, "Well, you don't have to hurry!"

I assured her I would like to come again, whether the Franklin church was reopened or not, and went back to Sullivan giving thanks for people like Aunt Minnie and a town like Franklin, nestled among the hills and gay with maples, blueberry carpets, and the incredibly blue September sky.

School had started again. Every day the big yellow bus with its eager load came up the road in front of the parsonage and turned around in the school yard just beyond. The little Scotts had somehow forced their unwilling toes into shoes, and with hair neatly plastered down, their grins as charming as ever, they trudged by the house calling out a cheerful "Hello, Minister!" They never did bother with my name. This year it was Orrin and Pamela who were starting. Every grade has a Scott child in it—all of them bright, polite, and clean. How Jean does it with twelve children I don't know. Each year she assures me and the doctor that this will be the last, and each year there is another one. The whole community worries except thin big-eyed Jean, old-looking before her time—and Stubby, her good-natured, imperturbable husband.

After school had been going two weeks I made the rounds, visiting each room. The teachers all said they would welcome a twenty-minute period of Bible story or religious discussion. It would give me a chance to know the children, because I couldn't get to the Sunday Schools. Very soon it became routine to spend Wednesday afternoons visiting Sorrento and Sullivan elementary schools and Thursday afternoons the schoolrooms in Prospect Harbor and Goulds-

boro. Armed with a picture and a Bible story I would make
the rounds. And what fun it is to go into these rooms. We
may not have the most modern up-to-date buildings and
equipment, but we have teachers of imagination and kindness. The groups are small enough so that everybody gets
individual attention, and for the most part I would say our
children are getting schooling better than that of many
city children.

I parked the car under the pines at Morancy school.
Morancy is a District all by itself. I understand that among
the families up that road anyone who lives along Route 1
or near the village centers is spoken of as "living outside."
About three families, with their various generations and
relatives, populate this District. The school building was a
two-room affair, the subprimary and first two grades in one
room, the third, fourth, and fifth in the other. They were
waiting for me, these children of the upper room. They had
seen me go into the lower room, had heard us singing a
song or two, and undoubtedly knew how long the story
would take, because when I went in their room I was met
by eighteen pairs of eager eyes and eighteen grins. They
could hardly wait for me to greet the teacher and tell the
story. Then the teacher said, "We have a question for you,
Mrs. Henrichsen. The children asked me, and I told them I
thought we'd wait and let you answer it for us when you
came. All right, Blaine, you may ask our question."

And Blaine came forth with this one: "Where was God
when He made the world?"

Well, we went on from there. One question led to another.
Mrs. Hooper had them put away their work when I first
came in and said that I could have the time until the bus
came if I could spare it. It was a wonderful afternoon. They

were keen, those youngsters. They had a smattering of information about prehistoric times and geologic formations and they were trying to think through a theology big enough to include their school information.

I breathed a quick prayer for guidance. It was so important that we give true answers—answers that were scientifically accepted, answers that gave a reverent sense of God in His creation. Answers that were not dogmatic but still definite enough so that these boys and girls would know that school and religious teachings were both true. Answers that would leave room for growth in their thinking. I knew some of the narrow interpretations that were held in some parts of our community. But I think we all felt it was as good an afternoon as we had ever had. I came back walking on air, ready to preach again on Sunday. These school sessions crowded the week, but how much they gave me!

"There's a man sick up on the Flanders Pond road," they told me. I had not been up that way, but one afternoon I went exploring. What a view out across the bay from that hill, the mountains rising out of the sea, the forest-covered points and islands, and everywhere the soft air of Indian summer, sweet with the odor of sweet fern and drying leaves. I turned in just after passing the beaver dam on Flanders Brook and came to an old weather-beaten house of fine lines standing alone in a clearing. There were geraniums in the windows and a small pile of slab wood near the entrance. Under the silver poplars, their leaves quivering in the soft breeze, lay an old man on a mattress. I knew this must be Perry, the man I had come to see. I sat down on the grass beside him. He hadn't walked all summer, he said. "I'm all right except for these legs," he assured me.

Presently his wife came up across the field. She had been out looking for a pig that had got away. I noticed a number of young shoats and said, "How many pigs have you?"

"Eighteen," she answered. "And don't they eat! With the price grain is it's all we can do to keep them fed."

"Couldn't you sell some?" I asked.

"Oh no. You can't get a fair price for meat these days," she said.

"Yes," said I, "but wouldn't it be better to take a loss than to have so much grain to buy?" But that idea didn't take root at all. She simply couldn't get a good price for her pigs, and she launched into a glowing description of how smart they were and how "knowin'." Besides the pigs there were two cats: a big tom with a baleful expression who bit and tormented the other, a fluffy Angora named Bounce. Bounce was her pet.

This little home so far from anywhere became one of my regular ports of call. There were few visitors; it was off in the woods and Perry didn't seem to "gain any." In local parlance he "fell away dreadful" and I managed to have a talk with the doctor about it. He agreed with my impression that Perry wasn't getting and couldn't get at home the care he really needed. I broached the subject of a nursing home. "Yes," agreed the doctor, "that's where he ought to be. I can get him in if you can persuade him to go."

So out I went again, perhaps two months after my first call. November had brought chill winds, the bright colors had dropped from the other trees but the hackmatacks were still a deep, burnished gold. The little house was cold. Perry's wife had told me that she couldn't have a fire in the bedroom because the chimney was cracked. When she had started a fire the roof had caught and they had had a bad time putting it out. With Perry's helpless condition I was terrified. Certainly there were not blankets enough in sight to keep him warm. The kitchen stove had a fire in it but it gave little warmth as the keen wind blew through the clapboards. Standing against the wall, I could feel the gusts through to my backbone. What would it be like when winter really came?

They needed water, so with her two pails I started for the spring, about half a mile down a logging road. It was a wonderful evening and fresh deer tracks in the road showed that a large buck and a smaller doe had gone together down that way. A late robin flew into a spruce thicket, a hermit thrush sang. There was a beautiful sunset, with orange and crimson lines that spoke of colder days ahead.

Back with the pails of fresh water, I had also found a conviction that her tired mind, confused and unable to plan, needed authority. So when I came in I said, "Now look. You can't possibly stay here longer. It's getting cold and soon there will be snow. The doctor says he can get Perry into a nursing home where he will be warm and comfortable and you won't have to have his care. Couldn't you go somewhere and board?"

"Oh I could go to my brother's," she answered, naming a city not too far away, "but what about the pigs?"

I managed not to say "Let's turn them into pork chops!" After all they were her pets. "I think we can find someone to take them for you," I answered.

"Well," she replied. "If you can—"

On the way home I stopped at the first selectman's. He agreed with me that they couldn't stay there. He had tried to get her to sell the pigs but had found her completely opposed to the idea because she couldn't get a good price. By this time I was sure it was because they were pets and she couldn't bear to think of their being killed. She was willing to go without food herself and to have her husband go hungry, but there was always plenty of grain for the pigs. The selectman assured me that he could handle the situation. "They've been 'on the town' for nonpayment of taxes," he said, "and we've given them a lot of help. We'll take the pigs as payment on what they owe. Then she'll have no reason for refusing to go, if you are sure her brother will take care of her. It will be better all around."

So it was arranged. An ambulance came and took the husband to a nursing home, where he was clean, well fed, and well cared for. The selectman took the pigs, and I went out once more to say goodbye to the wife, who was supposedly packing up to go to her brother's. I found her splitting a few slabs for her fire. "I thought you were going today," I said.

"Oh no," she answered. "I think I'll stay here awhile. I'll be all right."

I had to fight down a rising irritation. After all the trouble we had taken—the selectmen, the doctor, all of us working together to help her, her brother willing to have her—and now this refusal to go! I tried again. "It just isn't safe," I protested. "You know how cold that house gets and your chimney is in bad shape. Suppose you had a fire, way off here by yourself. And when the snow comes nobody will be able to get in to help you. And how will you get groceries?" She had been walking the three miles to the nearest store every few days, trudging home with heavy bags of groceries and grain for those pigs! Sometimes a neighbor came along and gave her a lift, but there were few people along that road. Often she had to walk the whole distance.

"Well," she said, "my brother said he'd come again next Sunday and he told me he'd take me then."

Was it just stalling? I couldn't be sure, so I said, "Well, I hope he does, and truly you must go with him then. I'm coming out on Monday and check up, and I hope I'll find you gone."

Monday proved to be an exceptionally hard day. There had been a late call the night before for serious illness. There had been a heavy program of calling on discouraged people all afternoon, and by the time I got to the turn it was beginning to get dark, the wind was rising, and I wanted to go home to my own supper and my cozy study. But I had said I'd go. So with a sigh of resentment against difficult and stubborn people, knowing full well I was more stubborn myself and would have acted just that way if I had been in her place, I went out, up the hill, around the corner, past the beaver dam, and into the little clearing. There were no lights. There was no smoke rising from the chimney. There were no plants in the windows. I got out of the car and looked in, just to make doubly sure that she wasn't still about, but there was no sign of life. So I gave a prayer of thanksgiving and started back for the car, when I heard a loud meow. I started in the direction of the trees where it had sounded and heard it again. As I approached the big hackmatack the old tomcat ran out of the bushes. This time the meow was more plaintive. I looked up, and there was the Angora kitten, her eyes glowing in the dusk. I could hardly believe she had been abandoned, she had been such a pet. Had she run off and hidden and the brother been unwilling to wait for her? Surely she hadn't been left to the mercy of winter and the wild things, to be easy prey for a great horned owl or a marauding bobcat. Groaning under my breath I said, "All right, kitty, I'll get you," and pushing through blackberry vines that tore my stockings, barking my shins on the slab pile, I managed to get to the foot of the tree. Kitty was just out of reach. I stood there coaxing—reaching up as far as I could. Finally she descended a little at a time until she touched my hand, then jumped to my shoulder, digging in with her claws. I got her to the car, where in a panic she cowered in a corner of the floor.

"What in the world shall I do with you?" I thought. Aloud I said, "Kitty, I can't take you home—my two dogs wouldn't appreciate you." I stopped at the cheerful lights of a farm where a widow lived whose husband I had buried a few months before. I liked Mrs. Hanna. She was a fine person, dignified, high-principled, and with sound common sense. She welcomed me and said, "Have you been to supper?" Her supper was over, her table spotless, her dishtowel hung behind the stove.

"I can't stay, thank you," I said. "I came in to ask you if you know of anyone who would possibly want a cat." And I told her my tale. She laughed.

"Well, I don't know," she said. "I've got two cats. Maybe my daughter would take her. Her two little girls have been begging for a kitty and as far as I know they haven't got one yet."

I thanked her and hurried out to the car. Poor Bounce was in a state of complete terror. I hurried down to the daughter's house, perhaps a mile away, and told my story. I talked fast and when Alta showed the least interest I brought Bounce in. Bounce promptly ran under the bureau and hid. The little girls helped. "Oh Mama, can't we keep her? Please say we can!"

Doubtfully Alta said, "Well, I don't know what my husband will say—"

"If he absolutely won't have the cat," I promised, "I'll

try to find her another home." And I fairly ran to the car
and backed out before she could weaken.

By that time it was so late I had lost interest in eating.
Weary of problem people and problem cats, I opened a can
of soup, heated it, and with a piece of toast called it supper.
I hadn't had much lunch either, but I was too tired to care.
I tumbled into bed to dream of cats that looked like pigs
chasing me through cold woods.

Not many weeks later the selectman called me. "Perry
died last night in the nursing home," he said. "His wife
wants to talk with you."

"All right," I said. "Where is she?"

"Out at their place," came the answer. So I hurried out.
There she was, more woebegone and confused than ever.
I didn't know how much faith she had but I could voice
my own conviction that the Father's love is never withheld
from His children and that Perry was safe in that love. She
seemed to respond and we made our plans for the simple farewell service that we would hold in the little church in the
village. Then, before I left, I told her about finding the cat
and what I had done.

"Oh," she said. "So that's where Bounce is. I wondered
what happened to her. When I got home that night she
wasn't anywhere around."

"What!" I exclaimed. "When you got home! Didn't you
go to your brother's as you said you would?"

"No," she said. "I just went to Ellsworth for the day."

I sat down on my chair again and laughed, helplessly,
hysterically. "Do you mean to tell me that when you were
away I came in and stole your cat and found it a new home?"

"Oh," she said, "I don't mind. As long as you are sure
Bounce is happy. Because now I will have to go to my broth-

er's—there's nothing else for me to do—and they've got a cat of their own. But you're sure Bounce is all right?"

So I promised to make a pastoral call on Bounce the very next day, and to let her know how the kitten and the family were liking each other. And when I called on Bounce I found the whole family devoted to her.

Perhaps this was a lesson not to act so impulsively next time—but I wonder. When I think of that pathetic kitten and the dark frightening woods, the chill November night and the cruel tomcat, and contrast her present home with two devoted little girls feeding her, cuddling her, taking her out in their doll carriage, I think maybe there are occasions when it is not too great a sin for a preacher to steal a cat.

FOUR

IN OCTOBER THE HOUSES HAD BEGUN TO TAKE ON A FESTIVE LOOK, as if they were all being wrapped in Christmas wreaths! Somehow the whole world seemed to be getting ready for Christmas. One didn't need a Christmas tree in the house when at every turn of the road they were growing, and after the first snow were decorated in shining tinsel. The effect of wreaths around the houses was due to "banking"—a necessary protection against bitter weather. Sometimes banking was done with "banking boards," but most of us had tarred paper fastened with laths to the lower clapboards of the house, earth piled against the lower edge of the paper to keep the wind from going underneath, and then armfuls of evergreen branches intertwined and laid thickly all around, making a snug covering so that none of the paper showed. My next-door neighbor added a beautiful row of tiny spruce trees close together across the front of her house.

Even the deer seemed to know the calendar. They had

been fairly tame all through September and October, one rarely went anywhere in the dusk or after dark without seeing them, but with the first guns at sunrise on the first day of November they had disappeared from sight, only to reappear in the dooryards, hanging pathetically from trees or barn rafters, or draped helplessly over car fenders as they passed through town. How there can be such slaughter year after year and still any deer remaining in this country, I do not see. Too many of our men had returned from overseas service with high-powered rifles, against which a deer had no chance at all, and with telescope sights and field glasses it becomes a sure slaughter rather than a sport. The legitimate hunting takes a heavy toll but the night hunting and hunting out of season is even worse. I have come to dread November for its spirit of slaughter and of lawbreaking as well as for its too numerous hunting accidents and tragedies.

On this particular December first as I turned the corner to go down to Prospect Harbor for evening service, an enormous buck crossed the road. His fine rack of antlers proclaimed his good sense of timing. Evidently he had stayed well hidden through many a November, but he seemed to know that on December first he was safe, especially when December first fell on a Sunday.

With the chill winds, keeping the fire going began to be a serious task, and calling had to be planned to bring me back to the house at least once every three hours to put wood on the fire. I found that to run the stove with a slow draft—the chimney damper open only a small way—was best for heat and most economical for the wood pile. I found, too, that small cracks around doors and windows could let in amazing amounts of cold air. Since the storm windows were not very tight and the front door had a good three-eighth-inch hiatus between door and door frame, there was plenty of fresh air in the house even when doors and windows were kept closed.

One morning I slept longer than usual and woke up to see a completely white world, with that lovely hush that snow brings. Even the school bus had been quieted by the soft whiteness. Dressing hastily I ran downstairs to see if the fire had held, and, as I reached the foot, stepped into snow up to my ankles. The powder snow had worked in through the crack over the door and lay in a white drift in the front hall. I slipped my feet into boots, put on my winter coat over my bathrobe, and went out into the shed for more wood, and for a dustpan with which to clear my front hall. "This is it," said I to myself. "Now the grim business of keeping warm and well becomes important." But somehow it didn't seem too grim—there was still the lingering sense of adventure and the remembrance that my ministerial grandfather had not only preached under just such circumstances but had brought up six fine children as well. And Grandmother had neither refrigerator nor electricity to make things easier.

By closing the door from the living room into the hall and from the kitchen into the hall, I had three rooms which kept fairly warm. The holes in the ceiling—my "central heating"—were also closed off, and so the rooms in which I lived stayed comfortable, but when it was necessary to go into the hall or upstairs it was like an icy plunge. Many a day that first winter I wore my overcoat in the house all day and kept my sheepskin-lined overshoes on, for the floors were cold in spite of the banking. And when the wind really got to blowing from the northwest it seemed to come right through the clapboards. Well, why shouldn't it? There was little paint to stop it, and the wood was dry and porous. Life more and more concentrated itself in the kitchen, and pastoral calling became a great joy, because almost every house I went into was warmer than my own! I learned all sorts of ways of keeping more snug that first year. The early settlers had made little narrow bags filled with sand just the width of the window sills—the sand was heavy enough to hold them in place and they did a lot to keep the cold air from sifting in. Old rugs were often folded or rolled against the doorsills, and a kettle, filled and steaming on the back of the stove, kept the air moist so that it felt warmer.

But the real test was keeping warm at night. A color photograph should have been taken. Once long ago, for a joke, someone had given me some long red flannel skiing tights. They were wonderful, though a bit strange under a pink outing-flannel nightgown. A blue knitted bed jacket, some heavy hand-knit white wool socks tucked into lavender hand-knit traveling slippers, a tan sleeveless sweater over the whole to add another layer and keep the underneath layers from shifting about too much. Never did a lady prepare for bed in such a colorful manner! And on really cold nights a blue sweater, pulled over the head, its arms tied around the neck, was the most comforting touch of all. That I had learned once from reading a sociological study of tramps. When "knights of the road" traveling in boxcars are cold, they take off their coats and wear them in this way around the head and neck. If the jugular veins and the nerve centers at the base of the brain are kept warm one is warm all over. I had never known why I read that book years ago, but this one bit of information has been priceless. The trick was to undress in the kitchen by the stove, then, opening

the door into the hall, make a dive for the arctic regions upstairs and crawl in under the big down puff which had been
one of my first Christmas presents to my husband.

By this time my family of churches had grown from the
original two to five, for the pastor of three churches strung
along Route 1 between my morning church and my evening
one had had to give up and the District Superintendent
had said, "Will you carry them until I can get someone
else?" I still have them.

Juggling the hours for so many different services has been
quite a problem. Gouldsboro and Ashville had formerly had
alternating afternoon services but both groups wanted to
have church each week. "We never know whether it is our
week or not, this way," they said. Gouldsboro liked the afternoon hour, Ashville didn't. They once had had a morning
time and felt aggrieved that having once given it up they
couldn't seem to get it back. But East Sullivan and North
Sullivan pretty well filled the morning. Of course North Sullivan really wanted evening—"It seems more like church in
the evening because that's when we always went." Prospect
Harbor had always had evening, too—and somehow that
made sense. These fishermen were out every day in their
boats and they had to have daylight time to oil and clean
their engines, though I found later that they actually did not
do much of this on Sundays. We managed somehow to arrange the hours and fit five services into the day, with East
Sullivan at ten in the morning, North Sullivan at eleven-
fifteen (which was much too close to the dinner hour they
assured me), Gouldsboro at two, Ashville at five (just
suppertime), and Prospect Harbor at seven-fifteen.

Between Ashville and Prospect Harbor was a farm homestead where I went for the most delicious suppers, home-made butter, cream so thick and sweet it had to be taken from the pitcher in a spoon, lobsters or salads or perhaps a slice of chicken, all of it served on pretty china, cooked by a friendly little lady who, with her brother and twin sister, maintained the only year-round guesthouse in the neighborhood. The hot rolls, the delicious slices of meat, the good coffee, prepared me for the final service with rein-forcements that added an extra note of enthusiasm to my voice. Such spots of luxury in this otherwise somewhat Spartan existence!

The little Ashville church sat on a high embankment at a curve in the road halfway between Gouldsboro and East Sullivan. East Sullivan was the oldest church of them all, a fine building close to the highway, too close for quietness, for trucks would grind up the hill in low gear and shift with violent bursts of noise as they reached the crest just in front of the church door. How I did wish the old idea of no work on the Lord's Day could prevail again. Not only does our hectic and nervous age need the peace and quietness of a true Sabbath but the people who worship need to be free from such terrible noise. The truck drivers always seemed to know when the pastoral prayer had begun and timed their worst noises to coincide. Back of the little church was the cemetery, with its delicately wrought iron fence and its grass-grown graves where blueberries grew big and sweet in the summer, now serene under its blanket of snow. East Sullivan church had the most upright pews I ever tried to sit in, appropriate to an upright people. No wonder they stood so straight, they could hardly have relaxed in such a church. The pulpit furniture that had originally belonged to the church was of black walnut—two delicate chairs and a little sofa covered with horsehair—but a later generation had substituted high golden-oak armchairs with red plush seats. On the center chair was a crocheted square with an eagle and the legend, "God Bless America." These chairs crowded the small, square, low platform where the black walnut pulpit stood, surrounded on each side by a little dark railing, and we were glad later to return the original furniture, which is far more beautiful.

The Gouldsboro church had a vestibule with one central door opening into it, from the vestibule two doors opened into the church, the inner wall curving outward between them. It is a church that taxes an undertaker's engineering ability when a casket must be brought down the narrow aisle, maneuvered through that narrow inner door, then out the central door. The church has a lovely simplicity. Maroon curtains made by the Woman's Society hang at the windows; the pews, not so uncompromising as those at East Sullivan, are painted white, and over the walnut pulpit hangs a large reproduction of Sallman's head of Christ. Close to the windows on either side, the spruce trees reminded us that this was forest country, and the little groups of worshipers gathered here with simplicity and reality of worship. Many of them lived "up the guzzle," which has become my favorite address in all America.

One night as I left the friendly farmstead between Ashville and Prospect Harbor, brother Bill said, "You'd better get the chains on your car. Big storm coming."

"How do you know?" I asked. The sky was dark and still, but it didn't seem different from many of these winter evenings.

"Them old hooty owls," he replied. "They was a-hollerin'

and a-hollerin' last night. When you hear them like that it always means a big storm."

And sure enough, two days later came the biggest snow storm I ever saw. "Them old hooty owls" had certainly known what they were talking about.

For two or three days the wind howled, the thick soft snow soon became dry and powdery. Whipped by that wind it stung almost like sleet, and drifted in great piles about the house. It drove like a white fog, reducing visibility almost to zero, making one glad to stay in snug and warm —or at least almost warm. One couldn't be really warm in the study where the desk and telephone were for the wind blew right through that wall, but by "holing up" in the kitchen I got along pretty well. The typewriter moved to the kitchen table. The oven door was open, and when I sat to read my feet rested in the oven. A wonderful time to get some of this study course behind me, I thought. But then, just as I was getting established comfortably, the phone rang. Marguerite's mother had had a turn for the worse! Could I get the car out of the garage? I had long since learned to leave the garage door open; better to have snow drifting inside than piled in a frozen mass against the door, making it impossible to budge. The snow-tread tires would do a lot but they wouldn't buck the drift across the driveway. Tying an old felt hat firmly down with a scarf around my ears and donning my sheepskin-lined boots and my winter coat, I took up the snow shovel and started out. As I opened the door the wind took my breath and tossed it a mile or so down the road. The storm door was wrenched out of my hand and blown back against the house with a bang that cracked the panels. This was a sure-enough blizzard! I managed to dig a crazy path to the driveway and tackled the height of the drift. It was hard work, shoveling against that wind, and I was well "tuckered out" by the time I had it carved down sufficiently so that the car wheels could do the rest. Stacking the shovel in the garage, I backed the car out and made my way through the gathering dusk to Marguerite's house. Their driveway had been shoveled by Marguerite's husband Maynard, so pleasant, so capable and so silent! One could hardly get a word out of him, but he was about as dependable a man as ever I saw, and so gentle with Marguerite's mother—strong to lift her, gentle in his understanding. Here was real devotion.

What amazing courage Marguerite and Phyllis had. They knew their mother could not get well, but the conversation in her room was as cheerful, hopeful, and robust as one could wish. I was there when the doctor came and followed him out to the kitchen. "It can't last much longer," he whispered to the girls. The quick tears were hastily wiped away, and when they returned to her room it was with a gentle teasing so genuine that even the sensitive ears and spirit of the sick woman could catch no undertone of anxiety. Seldom have I seen a family so gallant and courageous without the slightest hint of self-conscious effort or martyr-like resignation. It was worth the battle with the storm to be with them.

After my visit they followed me out to the kitchen and, closing the door, said in low tones, "We've sent for Mother's brother. He'll get in on tonight's train. Do you think you could possibly meet him for us? Maynard could go—but we don't like to have him away. He can do so much more with her than anyone else, and he's the only one of us who can lift her, and if anything should happen—"

"Of course," I said, "Maynard must stay here with you." I knew how they depended on him. To drive thirteen miles each way through that storm would not be easy, the train might be very late, but *certainly* I was glad to go.

So back I went to the house, found the biggest hardest chunks of wood for the fire, turned the drafts low so it would burn as slowly as possible, made a cup of hot soup, and started for Ellsworth. In the dusk the swirling, blowing snow made it almost impossible to see the road. The whole world was a muffled whiteness and only telephone poles or an occasional fence post marked the road edges. Cars were crawling along—and every little way one had slithered off the road, abandoned until the highway crews could get out the plows. A plow had evidently been through once but had scarcely made an impression. This was what my neighbors call a wicked night. The windshield wiper made a valiant effort to help the visibility but was almost powerless. Inch by inch I crawled—grateful when the light of approaching cars helped me to see the road limits. Finally I reached the station, to hear, as I had supposed I might, that the train would be about an hour late.

It came at last, and then the long difficult drive home. The trip should have taken twenty minutes; it took about an hour and a half, but we made it. I shall probably never have to drive under such hard conditions again. Fortunately, when we got back to the house the mother was still conscious and glad to see this brother. Their eyes, when they saw each other, made the difficulties of the trip seem like nothing at all. What a privilege to be allowed to share so intimately in family life that is robust and sweet and strong like this.

Almost any winter morning, after the ice on the bay has grown thick and strong, one can look out to see little tent-houses being towed along behind cars. Mounted on two logs, they are dragged over the white roads to be set up in what looks like a toy village—or a Swiss postcard scene—on the gray-green ice of the bay. With the snow-covered mountains for background it is as picturesque as one can imagine. Each little house has its own stovepipe and all of them are gaily colored, each one painted differently—not by design, but according to what paint each man had left over from some other job. The paint makes them more windproof and helps a man to find his own tent in snow or fog.

In these little tents the men spend their winter days, fishing for smelt through the ice. My neighbor Dwight tells me that it gets so hot inside they sometimes have to strip down to the waist, no matter how far below zero the weather may be outside. The smelt are taken through holes cut in the ice. Across this hole is laid a wooden bar, from which dangle about a dozen lines baited with minnows. In spite of the heat in the close little tent, it is an icy job for the hands to pull those lines up, remove the cold fish, rebait, and set them down again. When the smelt are really running, the men work as fast as they can, pulling up one line after another, and often make anywhere from eighteen dollars to sixty dollars a day. The smelt are taken on the incoming tide; when the tide changes the men often change the position of the house and chop a new hole. Sometimes a sudden thaw and shift of the wind will make the work quite perilous, and every once in a while a house is carried out on a piece of ice that has broken loose from the main floe. I wonder if people who eat the sweet little fish in New York restaurants wouldn't enjoy and appreciate them more if they could see these colorful little villages and know the risks of pneumonia that the fishermen take with the quick shift from the hot steamy little tents to the fierce winds and below-zero temperatures when they step outside between tides.

For several days I had been hearing mice. The little scritch-scratch in the walls was not an unfriendly sound, and although I don't like mice better than any other woman does, these dainty white-footed deer mice with their big ears didn't seem at all like the pantry mice of the cities. As I sat studying one night I glanced up to see one of these little creatures coming out from under my sink. It scurried across the floor, picked up a crumb, and darted back. Made bolder by that successful foray, he tried again. Soon another followed. I held my breath and watched. They disappeared again and evidently came up the wall back of the sink, for in a moment both were on my sink shelf. There was a bag of dog food there; one mouse would climb up one side of the bag until he got to the curve at the top where the heavy paper was evidently waxed and he couldn't get a foothold. He slid down again, backward. Over and over again he tried. Then the other little mouse climbed up from the other side. "The Church in Our Town" which I was trying to read lay unheeded, quite eclipsed by "The Mouse in Our Kitchen." Of course I knew I would have to get some mouse seed and get rid of them, but I hated to do it—they were so dainty and friendly. The trouble with mice is that they do gnaw and destroy, but that isn't so serious as the damage the wood rats do. But, even wood rats are not the horrid things their city cousins are. They are more like red squirrels with hairless tails—but they do come into houses, and especially they come in after mice. Occasionally a panicky squealing in the walls would indicate that one of these pirates was raiding a nest of mice. I had no compunctions at all about preparing a feast of rat-nip on crackers.

One night a tiny baby mouse appeared; scarcely more than an inch and a half long, it seemed completely fearless. Pinny, the cocker, was evidently aware of the slight noise it made scampering over the floor, and stood barking in the direction of the sound, but the baby mouse simply sat up and wondered what the fuss was all about. He was so tiny that he was below Pinny's range of vision, and evidently had no smell at all, for Pinny didn't see him and continued to bark, while the baby sat in front of him, not three feet away, and wondered at such a "towse."

Towse is only one of many words that were new to me when I came to this part of the country. I suppose they must have an Elizabethan or Scotch ancestry. They certainly are expressive. An "awful towse" is what an excited cocker spaniel can make at any time. I suppose it would be defined as a noisy fuss. I've heard mothers say to children who were making a racket, "Stop making such a towse about it." Another old English word that is current here is "gaum" and its adjective "gaumy." "He's kinda gaumy" is sometimes said of a city visitor who is awkward or clumsy in a canoe or in a woods camp. I was certainly "kinda gaumy" in learning to keep warm that first winter.

One of the loveliest things about winter here—aside from the clean snow and the sharp blue shadows, the glitter on every twig, and the deep color of winter sunsets across the bay—is the friendship of the little birds who come around the houses for food. My back yard was a constant fluttering of wings—peanut butter in the chickadee feeders kept the chickadees and nuthatches busy, and the downy and hairy woodpeckers. For variety there were doughnuts strung from my clothesline and the little birds would swing on them and peck away until there was only a thin thread of doughnut left. Blue jays, starlings, and gray and red squirrels made it hard to keep the supplies replenished for the small birds. Seed eaters were everywhere and I was glad I had left weed plants growing around the back door. Juncos and tree sparrows were there every day, occasionally wandering flocks of redpolls, almost always goldfinches in their quieter winter clothing, and along in February whole flocks of evening grosbeaks, resplendent in clothes that always managed to look like trim tuxedos with golden vests and neckties. What a sight it was—this flutter of black and white and gold! Sometimes there would be three or four handsome blue jays and sometimes the rosy white-winged crossbills, though we were more likely to have those in late summer. But always there was motion, color, friendliness whenever one looked out of the window.

That first year, every morning before the other birds arrived, two fat hen pheasants came around looking for split peas. My slim budget had to be stretched each week to include a large jar of peanut butter, a dozen doughnuts, a box or two of split peas (whatever hunter finally got those pheasants must have had delicious meat, for they were exclusively pea-fed, and what quantities they consumed!), suet, chick-feed from the grain store, and two kinds of dog food. What was left over bought food for myself. I began keeping bird lists and found it not uncommon to see and positively identify about one hundred and fifty varieties a year, even though this country is not on the main Eastern fly-way that stretches up the Hudson River and Connecticut River

Valleys. It adds so much interest to each day's travel through the parish to have one eye on flying things. It has also added to the nervous prostration of people driving behind me—for suddenly something would come into view and I would pick up the bird glasses beside me on the seat, stopping suddenly and without warning. The special guardian angel of bird watchers must have a busy day sometimes, but so far there has never been an accident, though probably the vocabulary of some of my followers has been increased!

In January the cold increased, though there was not too much snow after that first heavy blizzard. I found that the cylindrical stove in the living room would get red-hot—so hot that I was afraid to leave it. Night after night I would drop off to sleep only to awake with a start and go downstairs to see if things were safe. The baseboard of the wall behind the stove—though a couple of feet back—would be so hot you couldn't touch it, the paint blistering under the scorching heat. Surely this wasn't safe. I got a contractor to put asbestos sheeting around that side of the living room, but still I was losing too much sleep, so I took to sleeping on the old couch downstairs where I could more easily keep track of the situation. The fear of fire is always with us, and well founded it is, for with no town water supply, no organized fire department, fire once started has pretty much its own way. I had stood by and seen a home go to nothing in a few minutes, while the men of the town did what they could with Indian pumps and hose laid to a brook. I looked lovingly at my old family antiques and my pictures, books, and household treasures and felt the need to be always extra alert to fire hazards.

"You don't lack for books, do you?" was the comment

of one of my neighbors when she came in. I certainly didn't
lack for books. They were all over the place—three book-
cases in the study, a large one in the hall, another at the
head of the stairs—a small one in my bedroom—and books
on every table, along the edge of my desk, often in chairs,
and occasionally on the floor. No—I didn't lack for books.
I had had visions of long cozy winter evenings and days
when one couldn't get out, and knowing that I would be a
long way from a library, and being very conscious of the
need for resource material in connection with my studies
and sermons, I had bought every book I could manage that
seemed to be a necessary tool for the study course. Some
of my mother's old friends, interested in what I was doing,
had banded together as "Parson's Pals" and were seeing to
it that I had the books I required. It was a wonderful help.
A second-hand set of Hastings' Bible dictionary, found in
Boston, was an expensive investment but a reasurrance
against the questions that might be asked that a preacher
could be expected to answer, though it had nothing to offer
on "Where was God when He made the world?"

The trouble was not lack of books but lack of time to
read and master them. Those long shut-in days that I had
envisioned just didn't exist. The roads were kept plowed,
the parish calls were many, and there was always the possibility of a new bird. Besides, the white world, the gray-
green bay, the dark evergreens, the blue shadows, and the
dazzling sunshine made it hard to stay indoors even when
the wind was sharp. I did resent it, though, when the thermometer dropped to thirty below, a furious northwest wind
blew for days, the sun was veiled through high thin clouds
that seemed to strain out all possible warmth, and I had to
go next door to get those everlasting pails of water. With

boots and mittens and overcoat, a scarf tied around my head, I would start out with the pails, but the pumping was hard in the bitter cold, the wind whipped some of the water away from the spout before it could reach the pail and what slopped over on the way home froze on my ankles. When the road was icy there was always the possibility of slipping. Though I walked gingerly there were the average number of falls, none of them serious—for I am well padded—but with the consequent loss of water, more pumping to do, and more ice to avoid. After a few such days I began to take the weather as a personal insult and told the Lord I truly thought I had been tested long enough on that score!

But at night there were glorious and eerie northern lights with flaring green-white pencils and banners of light streaming up from the horizon. Sometimes they seemed to be all about us with a pulsating motion like wave currents. Behind them the night took on a deeper blackness. It certainly brought to mind all the Arctic stories and pictures one had ever seen. No wonder primitive people feared such things. I began to have a strange feeling about them too, as if they were indeed some awful portent. It almost seemed as if they were especially bright about homes where death hovered. They had been uncanny the night Marguerite's mother slipped away. Whatever they may have meant to Eskimos and explorers and imaginative folk, they were not welcomed by smelt fishermen or workers in the woods, for to these men they were an indication of "soft weather" coming. To all of us, however, they are a constant reminder that the secrets of the universe are not yet mastered and that this is still a world of beauty and wonder where man must learn how small he is and walk most humbly with his God.

FIVE

"I KNEW YOU'D COME—"

I was grateful that the pale big-eyed young woman didn't know how very near I had been to not coming. She had cancer. Her pain was just unbearable. It had been hard work, that day, to make myself get up from my comfortable study and go over to her house. She lived in Franklin, the town that didn't think the church could be reopened, but I had found out that the pastor of the other church didn't call there and had made it one of my regular stops. Some days she was fairly comfortable and in pretty good spirits. But this was one of her bad days.

"You could always have your mother telephone," I said. "You know I'll be glad to come any time you especially want me."

"I hate to bother you," she answered, then with a shy smile, "besides, God always seems to get you over here when I need you worst!"

Such simple faith, and how it helped! For like Effie, I too had my bad days. Not bad with pain, like her increasing agony, but with a sense of uselessness. These Down East folk are very slow to give encouragement. Many and many a week had passed without indication that my efforts to be a good pastor meant anything to anyone. Of all instruments the devil has at his command—and he certainly has quite a bag of tools—this one of making a person feel that he isn't really needed or wanted is the most dangerous, I verily believe. When sermons seemed flat and trite to me, and my spirits grew as brown as the mud and fog that were everywhere as winter began to break up, the best cure was to go and call on someone like Effie. Yet even there self-distrust got in my way. I wondered if I were exploiting her helplessness because of my own need to be useful. But the glow in her dark eyes and the flush of pleasure on her face were reassuring.

I stayed much too long. Each time I got up to go Effie urged me to stay a little longer. The odor in the room was pretty bad. Her mother did all she could to keep things clean and sweet, but this illness has its own special difficulties and the heavy foggy air that drifted in the half-open window seemed to intensify rather than dispel them. I marvel at the patience of these older women who have to cope with illness like this without running water or washing machine. What endless trips up and down stairs Effie's mother had to make! Her strong patient face was showing the strain, her heavy tread sounded the weariness of heart as well as of body.

That weariness had begun to work havoc in the family. The mother and the husband of the sick girl, out of sheer anxiety and fatigue, were having difficulties with each other. It worried Effie and when her mother went downstairs she talked to me a bit about it. She seemed to need to talk. But after a while she turned to happier topics. I had commented on the pretty bed jacket she was wearing. She loved pretty things. In her late twenties, she should have been enjoying them to the full instead of lying here with her long thoughts when the pain eased, her black struggles just to hang on when it was bad.

"Do you ever wear earrings?" she asked suddenly. "You'd look well in them."

"Why no," I answered, "I never have."

"Well you ought to. They'd be becoming."

Just then her mother came into the room. Effie asked her to get a certain box out of a bureau drawer. She opened it and took out two simple little pearl earrings. "I want to see you in these," she said. "Please put them on for me."

I stepped over to the mirror and screwed them into place. They did look well, certainly.

"There," she said. "I knew they'd be becoming. Now don't let me catch you without them," she laughed. "I'll never wear them again and I want you to have them."

Tears came into my eyes as I thanked her. But Effie wasn't through. It was on the occasion of another visit a month or two later that the talk turned to serious matters.

"I'm not kidding myself," she said. "And nobody's fooling me with all this cheerful talk. I know I can't get well."

I didn't argue the point. So often the pastor is the only one to whom a very sick person can talk about what is ahead. Why shouldn't we look forward eagerly to the greatest of all journeys and talk about it freely and happily?

"Maybe not," I said, "as we think of it. But this I know. You are going to be well—entirely well—gloriously whole and strong as you never could be in this life." So we talked a bit, easily, about the wonder of a life without the limits and limitations to which we have to adapt here. Then again her thoughts went to her pretty possessions. She told me what dress she wanted to have put on when she could no longer choose for herself and then she said, "I want them to put my pink beads on me, but after the service I want you to have them. You wouldn't mind wearing them—after that—would you?"

"Of course I wouldn't," I said. "I'd wear them proudly, always with a happy thought of our friendship."

"There are earrings that go with them," she said. "I've told my mother I want you to have the set—afterward—"

And so now, when I am really dressed up, I wear the pink beads and the earrings, but more precious than either is the memory of the reassuring childlike faith that somehow the Lord would get me over to her house when she needed me.

Of course I believe with all my heart that God does often do just that sort of thing if we are sincere in wanting to be used where He wants us. But I do not believe for a minute that we are puppets manipulated by Divine fiat in every move we make. There are amazing instances of finding ourselves in the right spot at the right moment. But there must also be many more times when we fail to be there because our own insistence on what we want to do, or think we ought to be doing, gets in the way of the gentle touch of the Holy Spirit. I cannot go along with the thinking of the lady whose car gave trouble on a back country road. It was a lonely road, but finally someone appeared on a bicycle.

"Are you a mechanic?" she asked.

"No ma'am. I am an electrician."

"Oh," she said. "Well, my car has broken down. If you are an electrician I suppose the trouble must be in the ignition of the car. The Lord wouldn't have sent you just now unless you could help me."

Utterly nonplussed at the logic of this, the man lifted up the hood and took a look. The trouble was in the ignition!

"I'll need a bit of copper wire," he said. "If I had a piece of copper wire I could fix it up."

"Well, if that's what's needed it's somewhere around," she said simply. She began searching the bushes and before long came on a coil of new wire left by the telephone company. A short piece of it, and the trouble was fixed. She loaded the man and his bicycle into the car and drove him into town. I wonder if he has told the tale as often and with as much delight as she has.

But I react against this sort of thing. God is not a celestial magician nor a heavenly office boy running around to repair our troubles and get us out of the fixes we get ourselves into. Nonetheless, every detail of life is in His care. "Not a sparrow falls but your heavenly Father knows."

Someone had given me some clothing to pass on to anyone who could use it. The dresses were very good indeed and very small sizes. As I thought which of my many friends might use them, I remembered Inez. She was about the right size.

It had been several months since I had called at their little house, way back off the road against the mountain. It was a road I didn't dare try in winter, much less in "mud time." This is a definite season with us and lasts from about the first of March, when the frost begins to work out of the ground, until well into May, when spring really shows green gladness along the roadside edges. It is a time of muted browns and grays. Fog, slush, wet snows that quickly melt, and mud everywhere. But now there had been another two or three days of freezing; the roads had hardened up again, temporarily. It would be safe to go.

The house is at least three miles back from the main road and two from a neighbor, except for an Indian couple who have a shack hidden back in the woods there somewhere. As the road comes out of the woods, where a bit later arbutus can be found, it crosses a bit of flat cranberry heath, with a little pond now well frozen over—and nothing but wild country stretching from there back to the top of the mountain that looms in the distance.

Inez has one of the sweetest expressions and sweetest voices I have ever known. She spends her life caring for a helpless husband confined to a wheelchair. His paralysis has affected his mind so that there is no companionship of thought, only a companionship of need and of love meeting that need.

Horace greeted me with his friendly smile. He has a sweet tooth and a love for pretty things. Once I had taken him a little religious picture in bright colors, and a bit of candy, but this time I hadn't thought to take him a present. Inez, though pleased with the clothes, seemed greatly perturbed. The Indian neighbor Louis had a dog whose paw was hurt. He was there at her house, had in fact stepped out of the house as I approached. The dog, a young black and white collie, was in great pain, the paw sticking out helplessly at right angles—obviously a bad dislocation.

"Here," I said, "you'd better get right into the car with him and I'll take you to the veterinary." (It was about twenty miles away.)

On the way over Louis told me how it had happened. The young collie was a great one for chasing small animals, good at catching rats and mice. He had chased a red squirrel up a leaning tree and then jumped from too great a height.

And that was the moment, out of all those months, when I had decided to take those clothes, which could just as well have been taken any other day—or even a few hours earlier on that day! How much we don't know about how the spiritual laws of the universe operate! This amazing partnership of a God all wise and all powerful who humbles Himself to work through bungling human hands in relieving the distress of His children and His little creatures, yet who will not override man's will to hurt and destroy these same creatures unless and until a man himself chooses the law of kindness!

How much of this incidental sort of pastoral service comes my way. I wonder often if it really helps the work of the Kingdom of God for me to take hours of time for such errands as being an ambulance for an injured dog. Yet how can one turn away from need? Besides, it is only the incidental and natural contact that I ever get with people like this Indian neighbor. They do not come to church; if I should go to call at their little shacks they would be embarrassed, would find it hard to talk with me. The wives would talk in monosyllables, the menfolk would simply disappear till I had left. But this way I had a chance for some real conversation with a man whose love for his dog was like my love for mine. We met on common ground. Maybe saving a dog pain has some relation to saving souls! I wonder.

That spring added another church to my growing family.

The high school youngsters had approached me one day after our Assembly period. "Will you come down to Sorrento to preach if we can get the people?"

"Of course I will," I said, "if we can find an hour."

So we planned to begin that Easter with a service at two in the afternoon. It wasn't the best time, but the people began coming eagerly and I was glad to have this little church in action. For a long time it had held services only in the summer, and part of the time only in the month of July. All the rest of the year the permanent residents of that little village had had no church. But now it was launched and since it is a village with a great many young families, a town that in a few years will be full of growing children, it is in some ways the most important church of all.

As Easter approached I found myself growing more and more concerned that this should be a really beautiful and significant service in the churches. When I asked about flowers, I found a rather vague response. "Well I suppose if anyone has a plant they could bring it."

"What about Easter lilies?"

"We've got some paper ones in the cupboard. We can get them out."

I was horrified—paper Easter lilies! It seems they had never thought of such a thing as spending church money for flowers. One never had "boughten flowers" except at funerals.

As I went around the parish talking with parents about having their babies baptized, trying to find those loyal and faithful souls who for years had loved and worked for but never joined the church, in order that we might bring them in at Easter time, my mind revolted at the thought of paper Easter lilies. I was sure I had to have real ones. How to do it without hurting any feelings? Although I had ordered them long since for the church in New Jersey where I had grown up, in memory of my parents and grandparents, I decided to have another memorial group of lilies here. I went to the florist in our county-seat town, a florist whose flowers are as fine and fresh as any big city florist's I have ever seen, and whose funeral arrangements were unusually beautiful. I told him about the lilies. He was most sympathetic and interested and made it possible for me to buy five beautiful plants with the amount of money I had expected to have to use for three.

Saturday afternoon, just before Easter, a car drew up to the parsonage door. A neighboring minister from the Seacoast Mission in Bar Harbor was there. "Could you use some Easter lilies for your services?" he asked with a friendly grin.

"I'd be thrilled to have them," I answered. He brought in two lovely plants. So on Easter morning the back of my car was completely filled with Easter lilies. I took them in to one service after another. A few of the blossoms got slightly bruised with all the taking in and out of the car and the jarring against the back of the seat, but they stood up to the ordeal wonderfully and made each church glorious with their heady perfume and their pure loveliness.

In the little Ashville church, as I arranged them along the edge of the platform, some of the children came up to smell, asking ecstatically, "Are those real?"

"Yes, they're real," I answered.

"Ain't they handsome?" I heard one woman whisper to another. Later someone told me they were the first real Easter lilies they had ever had in that church. We have had them each year since.

At Gouldsboro when I announced the hymn "Christ the Lord Is Risen Today," the organist whispered, "It's not familiar—"

"Never mind," I whispered back. "We'll sing it anyhow!"

Obviously it wasn't familiar. One or two soft voices murmured through it, trying to follow the tune. I sang loud and lustily. That hymn has been in every Easter service of my entire lifetime. What did they sing, I wondered as I let my voice go out on the Alleluia.

But it was a lovely service nonetheless. The bright responsive faces of those dear people, the fresh spring clothing, even to white gloves on the little girls and a new flower on older hats. Myrtle's honest comment at the end didn't bother me a bit. "That was an awful homely hymn you sang," she observed as we went out into the soft air where only the blueness of the sky gave a hint that winter had lost its grip.

It had been a wonderful Easter, churches packed as I hadn't seen them since Christmas, twelve babies christened, and such darling ones! One little girl put her hand on my mouth, making it rather difficult to pronounce the tender words, another made a pass at my hair, and one had echoed each phrase of the service with a little responsive "Unh!" just as if she were understanding the agreeing with it all. With these, and the four adults whose eyes had been so full of deep feeling as they took the membership vows, with the memory of the awed delight that the people everywhere had shown at "real lilies," with the chuckles at the comment on the "awful homely hymn," I was too keyed up to sleep that night—and when dawn came rosy and clear behind the dark spruces on the horizon I gave thanks that for me, too, Easter was the beginning of a new life among these dear people. I had lived through my first winter. The mud would go sometime, and the fog, and spring would really come.

It did, at long last, and every roadside for miles was embroidered with silver shining pussy willows. I knew I should miss the flowering shrubs of spring known in gentler climates—no forsythia up here, no azaleas, no laurel, but the silver of pools and puddles and little rivulets everywhere was taken up through the crimson withes of the willow bushes, to sparkle in the soft fur of the pussies.

One Wednesday evening when I was working on my sermon, I suddenly heard the wild bell-like honking. I dashed outdoors—the air was ringing with it. It seemed as if the Milky Way was shaking with the cry. I couldn't see the geese; they were probably coming into the bay just below the house. This was a late arrival, for usually geese find their places before dark. Perhaps this was a protest to a leader who wanted to go on through. But it was the sign we had been waiting for. Geese going north meant that before long goose-neck greens would be found in the marshes and that we were well on the way to arbutus, shadbush and spring peepers.

They told me that down the road was a sick woman who lived with her son in a little simple house near the site of the old wharf. I had seen the son—a grown man, excessively shy—come scurrying up to the store and then return to the house. He couldn't leave her alone at all. On the house was a sign, "Westclox." I was told that he was the best clock repair man anywhere around and that the jewelers in Ellsworth sent much of their work to him. I went down to call. I got no response to my knock. I knocked again, louder. After a while I heard a door close somewhere inside, then another, then footsteps approached, the front door opened just a crack. Behind the man I could see the inner door tightly shut.

"I'm Mrs. Henrichsen, the minister," I said. "And I heard your mother was sick. I'm so sorry. How is she today?"

"She's poorly, thank you, ma'am," he answered, still holding the door open a crack.

"Would she like to see me?" I asked.

"No ma'am—" It was very final.

"Well," said I with determined cheerfulness, "you tell her I asked for her, and if there's ever anything I can do I'd be so glad to do it. And I'll be down again to see her someday when she feels more like it."

I strongly suspected that every call would be just about like that. It was puzzling. I felt sure I could make friends if I could once get inside and have a chance.

When I got home I went over to the study bookcase. There was the solution—the antique clock that never ran. Not that I wanted it to. It had a loud tick that you could hear all over the house—a tick that reminded me of hot mosquito-filled nights when I was a child, sleeping, or wishing I could sleep, under heavy mosquito netting canopies on the porch outside my aunt's bedroom, where that clock ticked like an infernal machine. But it was a nice old clock. Surely it would serve as an icebreaker.

So about ten days later I took it down to the house. When I mentioned "clock" the crack in the door widened, Wallace saw it, and invited me to come in. What a neat housekeeper this man was. The house was shining, his workbench covered with tools, each in its place, the teakettle singing on the stove, and the room full of clocks of all sorts. He was interested in my old clock with its early date and thought he could put it in order. Again I asked about his mother.

"I'll go see if she wants to see you." And he disappeared into the next room.

"She doesn't feel like it today," he answered, but this time the tone wasn't so final.

"Maybe when I come for the clock," I suggested. "I really would love to meet her."

So when the clock was ready, they were ready too. They had had time to prepare for the ordeal of a caller. The house was even neater than usual, and the old lady's daughter was there for reinforcement. She was a very sociable person and after a bit of general conversation asked me if I wouldn't read something from the Bible. I chose the lovely "Let not your heart be troubled" passage, and left, feeling that I had scored a real victory, for as I went out the door Mrs. Holmes said, "You don't have to hurry."

These visits soon became weekly affairs. Always I would read a portion of my favorite Scriptures and always the little lady would say, "That's good." Although the son stayed out of the room when I was there, I noticed that the soft sounds of his work in the next room would cease when the reading began, and I think he came to enjoy the visits as his mother did. I came to value his regard, for he is one of the really fine people of this town. He has a craftsman's love for his work and shows marvelous skill and care in it. One of my neighbors took him a modern alarm clock to fix. He said, "Well, I'll fix it if you say so—but 'tain't worth fixin'—these modern clocks ain't no good—cheap metal works no better'n a threshing machine—"

But he fixed it. And when she went to get it he scorned all pay, saying, "No, course I won't take pay for fixin' that. 'Twan't worth fixin' anyhow."

He has a fine system for avoiding the complications and headaches that bother the rest of us around March fifteen. He simply stops short of reaching the income tax level. He could have all the work he could handle, but he keeps track, and when his income gets to the point where another dollar or two will make it necessary for him to make a declaration, he refuses pay for his work. When someone asked him about it he answered: "Oh, I'd do somethin' wrong and they'd put me in jail. It's better this way."

And maybe he's got something there!

When April nights are soft and warm and misty, over in the meadow behind the lawyer's house I can hear the woodcock. It is fun to go over and stand, though one must be rubber-shod, for the grass is spongy wet. When dusk comes a strong "beep, beep" note sounds from the edge of the wood. In the gathering dusk it is almost impossible to see the little brown woodcock, but when the beeping gets worked up to a certain pitch of intensity a bird will suddenly fly up, his wings making a musical whistling sound. The flight is incredibly fast. Spiraling up he gets very high, often out of sight, and then swings in great circles, singing a lovely bubbly song, like a child who blows soap bubbles with the bowl of the pipe upward. The song continues for several minutes as he swings around and then he plummets silently to earth, landing in almost the exact spot from which he rose. I had read about it all my life; now I was hearing it, the lovely courtship song of this strange, shy bird. Finally I caught sight of him only a few yards from me—his feathers blending exactly with the brown leaves and grasses of the marshy ground, his big round eye and his long bill giving him the appearance of a strange little dwarf leaning on a cane. Next to wild geese, I think the woodcock gives me the feeling of being close to the mystery of the Creator and the very heart of spring.

Then—about the first of May—come those sudden hot days that bring the arbutus to flower. The pinky-white waxy blossoms with their delicate fragrance are the delight of everyone. But how awful it is that they are picked with such long stems. Maine is not conservation minded. There have always been such quantities of these lovely things. I tried to tell the school children about cutting them with little short stems to save the creeping runners, but they looked at me as if this was another of the strange notions of the minister. They have always picked all they wanted. In fact, one woman told me of picking a pillowcaseful for a wedding some years ago. It made me fairly sick. Now we hunt over many places where they should be and find only an occasional plant.

These same hot early May days bring out the shadbush. Did I say I'd miss the flowering shrubs? No longer. Overnight the woods have become full of lacy whiteness—bridal veils caught everywhere between the evergreens. Wild cherry and shadbush make up for all the magnolias and azaleas and forsythia in the world, and by the time they have gone the bogland is ablaze with the magenta rhodora, and wherever there is an old cellar hole there are great quantities of purple lilacs. Wild apple trees, too, surprise us with their profusion of pink and white blossoms peeping out from some tangle and thicket. I am always glad to see many blossoms, for unless the tent caterpillars are too energetic it means apples for the deer in the fall, and the little brown ones that hang on frozen still have nourishment for winter birds.

Spring comes fast in Maine. Too fast. One day is still mud time—the next is hot summer, with the horse chestnut blossoms white candles along the road to the post office, the woods alive with returning warblers, and the leaves popping so fast one can almost hear them grow. No wonder there is the popular legend that Maine has just two seasons: winter and the Fourth of July!

Fast on the heels of the fading rhodora and lilac bushes come the buttercups. June is heralded by acres of buttercups —shiny gold beyond belief, snowdrifts of daisies, and the gold and orange patterns of hawkweed and Indian paintbrush. And here and there, in these Elysian fields, are blue lines where the wild flag traces the tiny watercourses through the meadow. All this color fairly shouts against the blue sparkle of sea, with its shoreline of pointed firs and wide sky of puffy white clouds.

SIX

ONE OF THE DELIGHTS AND COMPLICATIONS OF LIVING PER-
manently in the world's loveliest vacation country is that
all your visitors come at once. July and August remind us
that we are part of a larger world, in it but not of it. For it
is that which is different about our life here that attracts
them to us. I wish so much that all our people could really
understand and appreciate this. In some places there is a
good deal of rivalry and misunderstanding between "summer
people" and "natives," but here we are fortunate. Our summer friends are those who have been coming for years, some
of them for three generations. They belong to us and we to
them. We are interested in them as people, not as curiosities,
nor as sources of the very necessary income they bring to us.
They mostly like us for what we are, too, not just for what
we can do for them. Most of them own their own "cottages,"
and as summer approaches one of the regular sources of income for every able-bodied woman is "cleaning cottages."

Just about the time the buttercups are at their most glorious gold, the cleaning of cottages begins—about the same time the men "turn to" on house-painting and boat-painting jobs. The water system from Long Pond that serves the summer colony is turned on, and life shifts into high gear.

One of my earliest visitors that summer was a girl whom I had known in my Boston days. She wrote that she wanted to stop over on a vacation trip to Nova Scotia and I was delighted to have her. Her note said, "Shall I bring my trumpet?" Knowing that she was an excellent trumpeter, and feeling that some special music would add to our worship and create a bit of variety, I replied, "By all means bring it, and play a solo for us in each of the church services."

But the matter had slipped from my mind as the week of her visit drew near. I had planned to preach on sincerity in prayer, taking the Scripture from the sixth chapter of Matthew. As we started the first service of the morning, Virginia sat quietly beside the organ, her trumpet in hand, waiting for the time of her solo. I got up to read the Scripture, opened my Bible, and started to read, when in the second verse I came upon the words: "And sound not a trumpet before you as the hypocrites do in the synagogues." I did not dare look at Virginia; I choked over the words. The congregation began to smile—there was nothing to do but give in and grin and give them all a chance for a hearty laugh. In the subsequent services we began the Scripture reading at verse three!

A sense of humor is absolutely necessary equipment for anyone dealing with matters of human relationship, but it is a fearsome thing to have too volatile risibilities in the pulpit. On one occasion when the congregation were all huddled in the last three pews of the church I asked them, before the service began, if they wouldn't come down a bit closer and sit in the center of the church, that we might feel a bit more together. Then I announced the number of the first hymn, which had been selected early in the week, and found that it was "Draw Me Nearer, Blessed Lord." Fortunately that day the organist was absent and I had to play, so I had my back to the congregation. It took me three verses to get my face straightened out to present a proper ministerial gravity.

Dr. Henry Sloane Coffin tells of being asked to give an address at a very conservative Southern college. The Dean, who introduced him, carefully explained that though Dr. Coffin was then President of Union Theological Seminary, actually Union Seminary was not so radical as they had been led to believe, and that Dr. Coffin represented the more conservative element at Union. The Dean concluded, "After we sing this next hymn Dr. Coffin will address us," and then announced the number. The hymn was "My Soul Be on Thy Guard." Self-control is strained to the breaking point, sometimes, in the pulpit as well as in the pew. The illustrations in one or two of the pulpit Bibles were most amazing and no help to my dignity. I learned not to look at them as I stood before the open Book but to look beyond them to the great Fact for which they stand.

The summer people who come to this locality are wonderful friends to all the people, and they took the new pastor to their hearts with cordial warmth. The way they continue to attend church in good weather and bad, no matter how inconvenient the hour, is a wonderful tribute to their appreciation of the need for rebuilding religious enthusiasm along this seacoast. The first summer Sunday in the little Sorrento church, which had been reopened that Easter, there were a large group of these summer residents. I noticed a particularly tall, fine-looking man with his charming wife and three teen-age sons. From his clear deep voice, which led out on the responses and in the singing, I felt sure he must be a minister. After church he introduced himself as Dr. Van Dusen. Up to that time he had been simply a name to me. I knew him as the author of one of the books in the course of study. Whether this man was the same Dr. Van Dusen I did not know. So one evening I went to call.

Their delightful cottage, hidden away among the trees, commands a wonderful view of the bay and the mountains, and has its own little cove, where the boys have their sailboats. I found this was indeed the same Dr. Van Dusen, one of the world's great leaders of religious thought, one of the men whose vision directed the formation of the World Council of Churches, and a foremost leader in matters of church unity. I wanted to ask him to preach in the little church, but I knew deep in my soul that if I asked him to preach before I conquered the butterflies that rose in my stomach at the idea of preaching before him, I was finished. So I made a little inward vow that first I would conquer my fear of him. Those next three Sundays were torture of spirit. I was painfully aware of how thin and shallow my thinking must seem to him, how halting my leadership of the service, and at the same time, even more aware that all self-consciousness is sin.

Finally, on the fourth Sunday I actually forgot he was there and preached without self-conscious effort. It was a wonderful release, and then I felt free to ask him to preach. How gracious he was—speaking to all of us in the tiny church with his great human warmth, deep devotional spirit, and wide scholarship. We have become great friends, and after the second summer he asked me if I would spend a week of my vacation at Union, having the "keys to the city" and the right to visit any of the courses and attend any lectures I cared to. It has been a rich week each year to have the inspiration of such men as Dr. John Bennett, Dr. Knox, Dr. Walter Russell Bowie, Dr. Paul Scherer, Dr. George Buttrick, Dr. James Muilenburg, Dr. Reinhold Niebuhr, Dr. Paul Tillich, Dr. Samuel Terrien, and Dr. Davison. I have attended classes, soaking up ideas and information as thirsty ground soaks up rain, and the lovely welcoming spirit of the entire Seminary right down to the friendly porter has bolstered up confidence and courage.

Among other summer neighbors in the Sorrento Community are Dr. and Mrs. George G. Averill, friends of thousands of students on the campuses of Tufts Medical College, Colby College, Lee Academy, and the Good Will Home Association. Dr. and Mrs. Averill are of that blessed company who make giving a matter of intelligence as well as of heart, and whose lives are lived for the sole purpose of doing good. They have established the custom of inviting me to their house for Saturday night beans. The doctor's notes begin, "Dear Parson," and his comprehension of and sympathy with people in humble and difficult circumstances have taught me much. He is deeply devoted to the babies and little children of the community. Possibly the added incentive of an ice cream cone following church, which is one of his beneficences, has something to do with our splendid attendance of children at morning service. But they soon switch from the delight of that harmless bribe to the more grown-up point of view of coming because their good friend the doctor expects them to. He says that the most fun

and satisfaction he gets from life is in sending boys and girls
to summer camps run by the Y.M.C.A. and the Y.W.C.A. and
the distribution of "those pictures of George Washington on
new dollar bills at Christmas time." He remembers his own
boyhood when he adds, "There is a great thrill that comes
with the possession of that first dollar bill." One of his
favorite fictions is that he is "a heathen in need of conver-
sion," but certainly those legions who rise up and call him
blessed for the anonymous good that he has done interpret
the term "Christlike compassion" by a mental picture of a
spare, keen man with a twinkle in his eye, a slightly ruddy
complexion, and a passion for fishing. I suspect that he feels
very close to the Master of Galilee and remembers that the
first disciples were fishermen, as day after day he tries for
the salmon and trout in Tunk Lake.

That summer we decided to have a Vacation Bible School
for all the children round about. The school committee
were willing to give the use of the grammar school building and the school bus if we would pay for the gasoline
used. The bus driver gave his time for a two weeks' school.
Sixty-five children were enrolled. The school building was
next door to the church and so by having our work in the
school classrooms, our play on the playground, our nature
walks in the woods across the street, and our worship in the
church, we had a remarkably useful setup.

There were several who were willing to help as teachers,
but we soon found that in the teaching group was every
shade of theological interpretation from the most literal to
the most liberal. Basing the two weeks' study on the general
thought of Praise to God, we built the program around the
great hymn of Saint Francis. The children made notebooks
to illustrate it; the littlest ones sang it with motions. I am

sure the little arms coming up into the air as we sang "Thou rising morn with praise rejoice" and then the little fingers wiggling to represent stars at the words "Ye lights of evening find a voice" was an unorthodox way to sing the lovely old hymn, but it held their interest and they loved it.

One of the teachers was a "summer person"—an enthusiastic lady whose regular work was teaching in a progressive school in the winter. She and her husband were so delighted with the possibilities of this Vacation Bible School that when our two weeks were up they continued having the children who lived in their part of the parish come once a week to their place for an afternoon of religion and fun. The program was indeed remarkable. Seldom has a Vacation Bible School combined Bible lessons, hymn singing, and worship with sea chanteys and ballads, swims, suppers cooked on the beach, and even water-color painting and folk dancing. But somehow it held together, the children came to feel that God was in their good times as well as their worship, and that it was the natural and right thing to stop work and play to thank Him.

On the place was a tiny shack that had once been a pony stable and more recently a shed for lobster pots. The children cleaned it out and made a charming little outdoor chapel. As they decorated it they learned Scriptures appropriate to what they were doing. "The heavens declare the glory of God; and the firmament sheweth his handywork" was the psalm they learned the day they fastened starfish, which they had collected and dried, to the ceiling to represent the starry heavens. The little altar table of white birch saplings held a beautiful picture of Christ, and near the door was one of Saint Francis. One little girl, caught up by the reverent devotional spirit, wrote a hymn of her own and composed the music for it. They all brought bunches of bright berries, charming bits of driftwood, sea urchins, all sorts of lovely finds as their gifts to the altar. One day they found a gull wing on the beach—its feathers soft and pearly—whereupon they learned the bit about "If I take the wings of the morning, and dwell in the uttermost parts of the sea; even there shall thy hand lead me, and thy right hand shall hold me."

Whenever I visited I would be taken to the chapel to see what new treasures had been added, what new finds they had. It was a sight to see twelve or fourteen children come splashing out of the water and in their dripping bathing suits take a visitor over to see their own little chapel. They always entered softly and reverently. They would perch on the benches, talk gently of God's wonderful ways in His world, sing a Bach chorale or two, perhaps recite some Scripture, ask the visitor for a story, and close with a simple heartfelt prayer and the Lord's Prayer. It was not "playing church"—it was much more real, spontaneous, and genuine. Mrs. Hotson, with her inspired understanding of children, would enter in with them, guide and suggest, but never overdirect.

And after worship and swim (not usually mixed together in quite this manner, but so spontaneous and genuine that there seemed nothing incongruous about worshiping in bathing suits), the group would gather around the fireplace for cocoa and cookies. The afternoon would usually end with the singing of old ballads led by Mrs. Hotson's delightful husband, who accompanied himself with an enormous guitar, and the children joined in rousing choruses of chanteys such as might have been sung by their own seafaring ancestors. I think I have never known people who could so completely identify themselves with a group of children and out of that identity bring something beautiful and true.

One day I dropped in to find the group learning Luther's great hymn, "A Mighty Fortress Is Our God," by dramatizing it. The small boys were especially delighted by the feeling of warfare against evil and were delighted to impersonate the "world with devils filled" who were threatening "to undo us." They were very threatening young devils indeed, but when the Word was spoken they fell to earth and slunk away in a manner quite realistic.

And somehow after that summer most Vacation Bible School ventures have seemed tame indeed.

One day someone called me from a neighboring town. With understandable hesitancy she explained that her father who had recently died had for years worn an artificial leg, a well-made and expensive one. The family had felt it wrong to bury the leg with the body, for, after all, such things were not easy to procure and there might be someone else who could use it. Would I be willing to keep it until such a time, for I would be more likely to hear of someone who might need it than they would be.

I assured them that I understood and that I thought they were both sensible and generous in their attitude. "Of course I'll take it," I said. I could see that they wouldn't care to keep it around the house.

But my own house is tiny and closet space is small. Where could I put it?

The next day a car drove up and two ladies tenderly carried a long box into my house. I received it with proper gravity and with genuine gratitude that when someone had to meet the tragedy of losing a leg he would find a substitute available—if it should be the same leg and a person of the same height and weight. But I did wonder how long I should have to keep it! I carried the box upstairs and put it under the guest room bed, where it remained until the following spring, when I decided that the Red Cross Chapter would be more likely to find someone in need. But I have often wondered what bad dreams my guests might have had if they had known the contents of the innocent-looking box under the bed.

All too quickly the summer had gone and after Labor Day I settled down to the winter routine with a much clearer idea of what things needed to be done. But it was not until the third summer that we were able to begin on extensive parsonage repair. The roof needed shingling so badly that the churches decided to do something about it. I had appealed for five hundred dollars for this purpose and the District Superintendent had said that if the churches would raise five hundred he could secure a similar amount in missionary money for these repairs. A succession of baked bean suppers, fairs, rummage sales, and such finally provided our amount. As I mentioned the project to our summer friends, I got the amazing reply: "If you succeed in raising one thousand dollars from local efforts and the mission board, we will try to match it so you'll have enough to go farther with these repairs." I began to "see visions and dream dreams" about what might be attained with one thousand dollars.

Meanwhile the men had begun work on the roof. By the middle of October checks had come in to the amount of two thousand dollars from these blessed friends and we were making plans for plumbing. It was not a simple matter. It entailed drilling a well and finding a place for the septic tank. Since the house is built on granite ledge, that involved blasting—and blasting within six feet of the house. I had visions of the foundations being completely shattered by the impact! When I asked the plumber about it he suggested that I ask a certain man "who was good with dynamite" to take care of the blasting operations. I went to see him. He thought maybe he could do it, but whom would I get for the driller? It seems that the man who sets the charge doesn't do the drilling. I asked him if he could get someone but he thought I'd have more luck. He suggested one or two possibilities. When I went to see them they were away hunting. It was November and in November everything stops until the men get their deer. I finally got hold of one man after his day's hunting. Yes, he thought he could do it "after he got his deer," but whom would I get for holder? For every driller has to have two holders.

Again, he thought I'd have more luck if I asked them myself. It was exactly like the house that Jack built! Again I had to wait until they "got their deer," but fortunately the severe weather held off, and late in November, with the crew assembled, the place for the charge covered with heavy timbers and burlap to keep the rocks and dirt from flying too far, the word came. I got out of the house with the dogs, just in case, steeled myself for the shock, and then it came, with a roar like an earthquake and a great shuddering of the landscape.

Miraculously the dishes still stood on the pantry shelves and the pictures had not fallen. Truly "Cecil was a good man with dynamite."

All winter the great pit for the septic tank had blocked the passage to the shed door but since that door was seldom used it didn't matter. Imagine my dismay on coming home one day to see man-tracks in the snow around that side of the house. I followed the tracks and saw them disappear into the hole, which had completely drifted over. There were signs of struggle and floundering and, to my relief, more tracks leading away. Next day I discovered that the son of one of my neighbors, himself from another part of town, had come over to see if he could borrow one of my tools. Knowing nothing of the blasting operations, he had found himself neatly trapped!

Of course before we could embark on the plumbing venture we had to be sure there was water available. There is just one way in this part of the world to find out, and that is to employ a "dowser." I was told that in Gouldsboro a certain man was good at finding water and I went to see him. Yes, he'd stop by sometime, and with that I had to be content. But one evening his truck turned into the yard, and with his wife and daughter to watch he began pacing back and forth, a forked branch of apple wood in his hand. Over and over the same spot he went. Then he handed his stick to his daughter, for she too had this mysterious gift. He asked her to check on his finding. They agreed that one spot, close to the house in the north corner, had a vein of water. I asked for permission to try. Once before, in Plymouth, Massachusetts, where the water was close to the surface, I had tried this ancient and mysterious business and had been startled at the powerful electric shock that tingled through my arm and the way the stick had turned earthward with a force so strong I could not prevent its turning in my hand. But here there was nothing like that. I went over the spot they had found and felt nothing until I started to turn around in disgust. As I turned, the same tingle went through me and the dowsing rod pointed earthward. Evidently the electric current from a small stream so far below the rock was not powerful enough for me to feel until I set up some sort of magnetic field by the act of turning. Scoffers may claim mental suggestion, and surely that is powerful, but since I had never thought of any such possibility connected with turning around I cannot think it played a part in this. At any rate it is at that spot where the well was dug.

The following spring we got hold of a well driller and for weeks the hard clang-clang of the drill tortured my nerves. The well was drilled forty-one feet through solid ledge. Then came the problem of laying the pipes into the house. The plumber could not get them through the ledge below frost level so they were laid in a box filled with tar, which does not freeze.

At last the work was complete, there was a white sink in the kitchen—the outdoor drain was a thing of the past and water flowed at the turn of a faucet. I knew the thrill that was in Saint Francis's heart when he sang, "Praised be my Lord for our Sister Water who is very serviceable unto us and humble and precious and clean." Someday I shall have those words lettered and framed to hang in my bathroom.

Every good thing has its price, and getting the plumbing installed was no exception, for there were two plumbers in the town. It was the advice of the church trustees who had known their neighbors for years that the work be given to one. The other was hurt that the job had not come to him. He had been a regular church attendant for over a year and had been a valued part of the congregation. The entire family—the man, his wife, and four daughters—had lovely voices and had added much to the service by their singing. When the work was contemplated I had asked for estimates from both men, but with the war shortages of materials it was difficult to make any sort of estimate, and this plumber had never submitted one. When he found that the contract was not to be his, he and his wife walked out of the church business meeting and have never taken an active part since that day. The two older daughters were married by out-of-town pastors and the warm and friendly relation that we had had has never been entirely repaired. Surely there must have been a way to avoid such a break but I was not smart enough or surrendered enough to the Holy Spirit to find it. For a long time there was a place of pain in my heart whenever I passed their house, and an ache when I saw the distress in this man's eyes, for no one can carry bitterness in his heart and be happy. If I were the pastor I should be I would have found the way to help him, but the door remained shut a long time. Some things must wait for the mysterious ways of God, whose timing is not affected by our human impatience.

Late summer here is a time for family reunions. From great distances they come. Never before had I, whose life had been lived mostly in suburban areas, known of country where you could tell from a man's name where he "belonged." A man may live for fifty or sixty years in Connecticut or Massachusetts or some other foreign place, but he "belongs" in Sullivan, Franklin, Gouldsboro, or whatever. It was confusing at first. I used to hear people who lived in Sullivan say they "belonged" somewhere else, but after a while I realized this tribal spirit. For generations Tracys and Youngs have come from Gouldsboro—and now, when I meet that name, I shall be very sure that its ancestors knew these roads and hills. In a similar way Franklin was populated by Blaisdells, Bragdons, and Bunkers, and Sullivan by Gordons, Haveys, and Robertsons at the north end of town and by Beans, Martins, and Prebles, Farrins, Uranns, Hannas, and Johnsons at the other end.

Family reunions were times of great feasting: baked beans and "covered dishes," salads and hot rolls, pies, always apple, custard, squash, berry, and lemon, and in the fall mince as

well—and cream cake! There may be better cooks in the
world but I doubt it. Once or twice I have been invited to
join these reunions, to lead in a service of thanksgiving and
memorial for those who have gone before and ask the blessing on the family at the "groaning board." The meal that
follows is sumptuous reward for what little contribution I
can make and the stories and reminiscences of older days are
fascinating. I love to hear of "Uncle Eben" or "Aunt Casselina," who were "great hands" to do this or that. It was at
such a gathering that I picked up the story of a forefather
who went out to Portland for a visit and came back with
amazing tales of how things were done in other places.
"Why they even fried their eggs in water and they tasted
just as if they was biled."

The first names used here show originality and often a
strong sense of music. We have Devina, Bellva, Odessa,
Lovina, Sophronina, Menilvia, Casselina, Selena, Zelda, Zil-
pha, Truena Velzora, and Zida Lydine. Among the men the
names often have classical dignity: Dallas and Harvard,
Pearl and Ivory, Austin, Adelbert, Dwight, as well as the
more usual ones.

And as these names are handed down from one generation
to another, they carry a sense of rootage and stability. This
is not a land where the new and temporary easily supplants
the old and tried. "What was good enough for my father is
good enough for me" may be poor philosophy when it comes
to plumbing, school systems, and teachers' salaries, but it is
a good brake upon our too reckless and wasteful headlong
living. And many things that were good for our fathers would
be better for us, if along with the older slower ways we
would recapture the meditative faith and sincerity of worship which those slower ways encouraged.

SEVEN

FIRE IS ALWAYS A THREAT IN THE COUNTRY. THERE HAD BEEN heavy rains in April and May. It seemed incredible that the ground was so powder-dry by mid-July. Wells were low. My beautiful new bathroom had become an ornament rather than a working unit in the house. Fortunately we still had the primitive arrangements at the back of the shed. But clean running water had spoiled me for the rust solution from the next-door pump, so I took to using the car and going with pails and jugs to friends at the other end of town who had a summer supply pumped from Long Pond. Twice a day two pails and two gallons jugs would jingle down the road with me about four miles—and slosh all the way home. One learns some things about physics the hard way. One of the facts I learned was that a floating chip of shingle in the pail would create surface tension enough to slow up the sloshing from the car motion. Very little water spilled over when there was a shingle in the pail.

One morning I was awakened by an ominous crackling noise. I couldn't smell smoke or see anything, but the crackling was frightening on the still air. My first thought was the garage and I ran downstairs to look out of the window on that side of the house. There was no visible smoke, no sign of trouble. The thick woods below the house seemed all right. The noise sounded very close. It was mysterious. Going out to the shed I looked from the window to the south and saw flames shooting high into the lower branches of a tall spruce just two houses below mine. There was nobody in sight; the house between was empty. The people in the house where the tree was burning were evidently still asleep and unaware. The whole front end of a small shed near the tree was already gone. Here was the making of real trouble for the whole neighborhood in a matter of split seconds. I dashed to the telephone, told the operator, and raced back to get into some clothes. By the time they were on and I had come downstairs again to grab my water-tank extinguisher, a dozen men had been summoned.

Indian pumps from all over town were coming and in less than an hour it was out and there was no further danger. But another ten minutes could have meant a holocaust, for buildings and roofs were tinder-dry and houses stand close together along here. I shudder to think what it would have meant if a flaming branch from the top of that tree had fallen on the house. I gave thanks for super-acute hearing that could wake me, asleep on the other side of my house two houses away, with no windows on that side of the house.

A few days later, looking out from the back window upstairs, I saw an unusual amount of smoke rising from Mount Desert Island. It was in the vicinity of the town dump over there, where we often saw a column of smoke. But this was thick and black, rolling up in great clouds. I called the attention of the men who were working on my roof. "Looks bad," they agreed. It did.

Sometime earlier the chimney cleaner had discovered that my chimney had loose crumbling bricks near the top and mortar rotten with age. It needed pointing up and more—it needed rebuilding from the second story up. As far as anybody knew it had never been rebuilt in the lifetime of the house, and while I had not had any chimney fires, there was reason to suppose that some of my predecessors may have had them. At long last we had got hold of the mason who had promised to come all summer. The chimney was torn down to the second-floor level and rebuilding had begun. The blazing sky shone through the gaping hole.

I watched that smoke increase on the Island with mounting dread. There were a dozen or more fires reported in this part of Maine. The air was thick with the sickish-sweet smell of it, and I thought of the fern, the cedar, the spruce—all the lovely wild things that were contributing to that dread incense, and of the panicstricken small things of fur and feathers who must pay the price of man's wicked carelessness in the woods. There was a raging fire, they said, over at Spring River Lake not far away to the north; a small fire had been discovered in our own woods on Monday and the men were keeping a constant patrol. It was in a patch of woods at the head of the village street, less than a mile from my house. These old dry frame houses would go like tinder if that fire ever got loose, fanned by the steady burning winds that blew right down from the northwest. And the smoke from the Island spread each day, covering an ever larger area. The sky grew murky, the sun seemed a pale moon through the pall. I should have been passionately grateful for a pouring rain, even though it would have soaked everything I had, with that open hole in my roof.

Each day reports grew worse. There were fires all around us. I went out to call at the home of an old couple who lived at the edge of town, not more than six miles from the edge of the Spring River Lake fire. They were apprehensive and seemed to feel a bit safer when I told them that if there were any dangerous shift of wind I would be on their doorstep with my car. It was a real possibility that our whole town might have to be evacuated. When I returned home that evening I did some serious thinking about what few things of my own were essential and irreplaceable, and packed two suitcases. It was easier to pack then than it would be under the excitement of actual danger. Besides, if danger really struck I would have no time to think of myself—I'd have to be getting other people out. So for ten days those suitcases stood by the front door, ready to grab at a moment's notice. Sometimes I would need something in them. It was like living in a hotel room in your own house. Each time I left the house I wondered if it would be there when I got back. The heavy smell of smoke increased, the murkiness was everywhere, and the hot merciless wind continued steadily.

In spite of the fire work must go on, and that was the week when we were supposed to be having "Quarterly Conferences"—church annual business meetings. There were reports to prepare, supper meetings to arrange, people with whom to confer. Sometimes it seemed as if the people who had well-kept records had no telephones and the people who had telephones had no records. Anyhow there was much to do. The Thursday of the Conferences arrived, and with it the District Superintendent and his wife. We had a noon luncheon meeting in one of the churches and then returned to the parsonage. The Superintendent had been in northern Aroostook County the day before and had driven most of the night, so in order to give him a quiet house for a nap, his wife and I went out in the car. "We have about an hour and a half," I told her. "Where would you like to go?"

She named a certain point, an estate of one of our summer families of which I had often spoken to her as a place of special beauty. We drove down there. While we stood looking out across Frenchman's Bay to the Island with its heavy curtain of smoke, the dry leaves at our feet began to whirl as a vicious little wind sprang up. I looked up. Overhead was as evil-looking a black cloud as ever I saw, a baby twister blew across the land, whirling leaves and dry grass, whipping branches. With horror I realized that the direction of the wind had changed and that the fires which were still out of control would be driven straight toward the center of Bar Harbor.

I didn't want to alarm the Superintendent's wife, but with panic tearing at my heart I drove home. The Superintendent had wakened and we went up to the "vestry," where the women had prepared a fine covered-dish supper. I went out into the kitchen. Everyone was speaking of the fires in low tones: the possibility of the fire in our town, not a quarter of a mile from that very spot, being stirred up by this sudden wind, the increasing threat of the other fires, the threat to Bar Harbor. But we said nothing out loud and went ahead with our meeting. After a delicious supper of meat loaf, vegetables, salads, and pie, standard church-supper menu the world over—except when it is beans—we cleared the table and began the business session. Increasingly, gusts would shake the building. People looked furtively and apprehensively at each other, shuddered, yet kept their minds on the business at hand. Our treasurer hadn't appeared, the most important member of the group. We knew why. Her uncle, to whom she was devoted, worked in Bar Harbor. She was undoubtedly trying to get news of him. She came in late, white-faced, and made her report. The District Superintendent, unaware of the anxiety throughout the room, spoke his words of encouragement about the work, thanked the ladies for the supper, picked up his papers, put them into his briefcase, and went out. It was then about seven o'clock. We had another meeting scheduled for seven-thirty in Sorrento.

As we drove down to Route 1 where we could see across the bay, we were horrorstricken. A sheet of bright flame lit up the whole landscape. It looked as if all Bar Harbor were ablaze. The light was so bright that we could see individual houses outlined, though they were twelve miles away across the water—thirty-five miles away by land. We felt sure there could be no further meeting that night, everyone was out watching the fire. We hurried down to the Community House—someone had been there and turned on the lights. We went down to the shore—the community was there, the men already launching their small lobster boats to stand by and take people off the island by water if necessary. Rumors were coming in via radio that the only road from the island had been cut off. The women were beginning to plan for the housing of refugees. I told the people I'd take the District Superintendent and his wife back to their own car parked at my house and return to help set up emergency headquarters in the Community House. But by the time I got back it had been decided by Red Cross officials that all relief work had better center in Ellsworth, the county seat.

Refugees were housed there and in Bangor, from which places departures could be arranged to other sections if necessary. The District Superintendent hurried home to keep in touch with the situation regarding the church in Bar Harbor, and I went back to see the treasurer, who still had no word from her uncle. He was an elderly man with bad cardiac asthma. Her fear was that the smoke and excitement would cause his collapse even if he escaped the fire.

But toward midnight she heard that he was safe in Ellsworth and went over to get him, and I came home, but not to sleep.

It had all started, they said, from a fire in the dump that got away from those who were supposed to guard it. Acres upon acres of beautiful forest destroyed. Now, six years later, there is again a soft covering of green upon those hills where grass and fern have taken foothold and where little bushes are beginning to grow—but it will be a hundred years before the hills are forested again and then the growth will never be the same. For they tell me that after the spruce and balsam are burned off, hardwoods take over. The glory of autumn coloring will be increased but the lovely pointed firs, so picturesque and rugged, are gone forever.

Fortunately, the other side of the Island escaped destruction, and all through this country communities have become more concerned to have some organized protection available. Sorrento has bought itself a pumping engine and organized a volunteer company. I wonder how many such summers will have to come and go before our town becomes organized to have a water supply. In the hills above us are at least three abandoned quarries full of spring water, quarries from eighty to one hundred fifty feet deep, water enough to supply hydrants all over town with only the simplest sort of pumping and filtering necessary. Or the Long Pond reservoir could be tapped and pipes laid. How we need the vital leadership to push such a project. Insurance rates are prohibitive now. Each spring and fall we have epidemics of low-grade infection, a sort of mild dysentery which is referred to as "this distemper that's going around" or sometimes "this horse ail." I feel certain it is caused by surface water getting into the wells in the spring, low water in them in the fall. We lose garden crops from drought and are helpless when fires strike our homes—and all the time the means of safety is within our reach! I love the peaceful unhurried tempo of rural life but sometimes I long for a bit of urban aggressiveness.

Fire is terrifying whenever it gets out of control. I think it was most pathetic on one afternoon when I saw car after car and truck after truck racing up the street. Must be fire somewhere, I thought. Just then the red truck from Ellsworth went by. I called the operator to ask where, in case I could be of use. She told me the house and went back to her busy board, calling every man she could reach in town. The home was that of an old man whose wife had died the year before. It was just up the street a little way—less than half a mile. I walked up and stood with the others, helplessly, as we watched it burn. The men had been able to get a few things out of the front end of the house, but the kitchen was a mass of flames when they had arrived. Nobody seemed to know where Hollis, the owner, was. Finally I found someone who said he had gone to Ellsworth that afternoon and knew nothing about the disaster. I knew then what a woman pastor's job was in that circumstance. I couldn't help the fire fighters, but I could intercept Hollis when he came home and stand by him as he learned the news. I might keep him from learning it too abruptly. I called a lawyer in Ellsworth to see if he could find him. He had heard about the fire and had already tried, but said the aged man was on his way home. It wasn't long before I saw his car coming up the street. I had gone down as far as the store to meet him so that he wouldn't see the house before he saw a friend. I waved his 1931 Oldsmobile to a stop. His gentle smile lighted up a face that fairly shone with goodness, and he climbed down out of the car, evidently thinking to go into the store. It was hard to tell him gently and make him understand. With shock and unbelief he started toward the smoldering ruin, and then, as realization struck him, broke into sobs. Other friends rallied around. Before very long he got hold of himself and went to see what few things had been saved. Among them was his wife's sewing machine. She had died the year before and the little house held all the associations of sixty happy years.

He came back to the parsonage with me and after he was steadier he managed to eat a few bites of a simple supper and drink some strong hot tea. Another neighbor had already notified his only daughter, who lived upstate. I found some of my husband's old pajamas and wondered how this tiny, spare man, now so broken by this second grief, would manage to keep them on, for my husband had been a big man; but at least he was secure in the guest room for the moment. In the morning his daughter and her husband arrived and before they had even seen the ruin they assured him they would rebuild the house.

Lesser folk would have said "Well, you'll just have to live with us now. You ought to anyhow, to be safe." But not these people. They understood how a man's heart can be where his life has been lived, among familiar associations, surrounded by precious memories. They knew how very hard it is for older people to adjust to a new life. And so they convinced him that they wanted a little house at exactly that spot to come to on their vacations. By next spring he was proudly supervising the building of a little cottage that stands on the old site, when he could tear himself away from his fishing. At eighty-one he still had secured his fishing license and spent much time whipping the icy brooks for trout.

The water shortage brought its amusing moments as well as these deeply tragic ones. When I had first come to town I had seen the children going up the road away from the sea with their bathing suits.

"Where do you swim?" I asked.

"The To'dole," they answered.

"What?"

"The To'dole."

I was mystified. Finally somebody explained that Toad Hole was the name for the abandoned quarry. Tired of skimpy washes with my limited supply, I followed them and with my bathing suit and towel and cake of soap went up to the "To'dole." It was a wonderful place, a small lake surrounded by young birches, with veery and hermit thrushes singing in the treetops, and the calm sunset reflected in its stillness.

Presently the stillness was shattered by the sound of a jalopy and a group of boys arrived, hot and grimy from their day's work. Others showed up, girls and boys, little children and grownups, and we all swam together companionably. The water was clear and terribly deep, no place for beginners. A sloping ledge of rock about eighteen inches wide led from the quarry edge down into the water. Once off that ledge there was no footing until one found it again. The older boys had a natural high dive from the quarry rim high above us—the younger ones and the women and girls stepped in off the ledge. Clinging to it, we soaped under our bathing suits—then swam out into the quarry to rinse off. It was definitely community washday and a welcome one. What happens to people in dry countries who have no To'dole? The bushes near the quarry edge were draped with various articles of clothing brought along to wash in the soft water.

While we were there a truck drove up with great gasoline or oil drums which were filled with water to take back to various homes. We may not have the conveniences of modern plumbing in the country, and some of us who do have them are occasionally temporarily without water, but there is plenty around for those who are willing to sacrifice privacy for the sake of cleanliness and nothing brings a group of people together more quickly than a common bathtub. What a special luxury to have it tinted with sunset, overarched by the evening sky and edged with young birches.

EIGHT

SOME OF OUR PEOPLE HAVE A SHYNESS IN REGARD TO MONEY that is remarkable and restful in this commercial day. The milkman comes whistling, and with a leisurely gait, willing to stop and chat every day except payday. But the first of the week, when he presents his bill, he moves up to the house almost furtively, as quietly as an Indian, and makes his getaway, leaving the slip under the milk bottle. I seldom see him until I hear the motor starting up to leave. I think he must put the truck into neutral before he reaches the house so he can glide to a silent stop. If I do manage to see him and call him back he will smile and say, "Never saw women so eager to get rid of their money."

It is, I think, almost a game with him. I suppose he likes leaving the bill and feeling that then we can pay at our own convenience. His wife collects fifty-cent pieces, and so if the payment is made with those he'll shake his head and remark that he doesn't get much of that week's pay. "Funny thing,"

he said one day, "if they start paying me in bills on Monday I'll have nawthin' but bills all day—if they start giving me change it's just the same—pockets'll be so heavy by the time I get home I can't hardly walk straight."

I had a chair done over by a neighbor whose upholstering is as good as one would find anywhere. He measured and estimated the cost of material at thirteen dollars and sixty-nine cents. "Call it thirteen dollars," he said.

"Now look here," I protested. "You can't build a business that way."

"Well," he replied, "I don't aim to make money off people as poor as I am."

I thanked him from the bottom of my heart—and gave him thirteen dollars and fifty cents. He still was doing the generous thing by me, and my own conscience felt better. He was the one who, when we were discussing whether to use a certain material or one not so good, quoted someone he had known as saying, "I'd rather wince once when I pay the bill, than wince every time I look at it."

Another time, when I was buying some records, the owner of the store took a substantial amount off the bill, and when I again said, "You're not going to get rich at this business that way," he replied perfectly seriously, "We don't have to have as much as a lot of people to be happy."

It will be a sad day for rural New England when this spirit goes out of it.

Our town had no library but there was a little house, centrally located, standing idle and I knew the owner had a real interest in everything constructive for the town. There was a young woman who had a great desire to be of service to children and to people in general, but who had never found her niche. She had had some money left to her and was in a position to volunteer her services, and she needed to be busy. I knew there would be plenty of books available if it became known among our summer friends that we were considering a library project. So one day a group of people were invited to meet at the parsonage—people who, I knew, had the community's interest at heart and a love of books and reading. The five who came seemed genuinely interested, Betty was glad to give her time, and so I said, "Well, I have no more right to do this than anyone else, but somebody has to start it. If you are willing to serve, we'll appoint you the library board."

The project took hold immediately. The women held a rummage sale and made money for lumber—husbands were pressed into service to put up shelves and paint them. The rooms were freshly papered, effective paper curtains were hung at the windows, and presently we were ready for the opening of the Frenchman's Bay Library. Books came pouring in and the whole board helped our librarian classify and catalogue them. She prepared lists for the teachers at the school of those volumes which might be helpful to pupils in certain subjects. Before the opening day we had 800 excellent books, at the end of the first year 1200 volumes, and now the list has grown to about 3000. There is surprisingly little that is out of date or useless. When the library was ready to open we held a tea, bowls of fresh flowers were everywhere, the books were neatly arranged, and tea and cake were served to all comers. Two years later our volunteer librarian "graduated" into a professional library job in one of our larger cities, and another volunteer took over—a woman of large heart, well-read, and with many capacities that needed fuller expression than her life had hitherto provided. At a subsequent

Town Meeting the library was "accepted" and now, each year, one hundred dollars of town money is appropriated for its maintenance.

There are stories of this country that should be in that library. There is the story of the preacher, one Reverend George W. Adams who lived in Jonesport, about fifty miles east of here, whose zeal led him into interesting endeavors. He led his people into a communal experiment known as Shiloh and built a "temple" of good pine boards around which the community life centered. But the most famous tale is that of his expedition, with a number of his followers, to "free the Holy Land from the Turks." It was in the year 1862 that this crusade took place. They set out from the little harbor of Jonesport with a high and holy zeal, and in square-rigged ships crossed the Atlantic and eventually made their way through the Mediterranean to the port of Jaffa. There they found that the Holy Land had no desire to be set free from anybody, and seemed to be getting along very well indeed as it was. So they turned around and came home— all except one enterprising Yankee who thought the transportation facilities from Jaffa to Jerusalem needed to be improved. He stayed on and set up a sort of taxi business with donkeys, and prospered from the business of Jews, Turks, Arabians, and sundry travelers from all parts of the earth.

And there are earlier stories, among them the tale of Daniel Sullivan, patriot, from whom our town takes its name and whose grave lies in the woods below the schoolhouse. He was captured by the British in the Revolutionary War and taken to Halifax as a prisoner on a British ship. I wish I knew more of his story—and the story of one of the early Frenchmen for whom our Frenchman's Bay is named. He arrived with Monsieur de Cadillac and chose an Indian girl for his wife. But unlike many of that day, his standards were such that he would not take her in common law marriage, but went sixty miles by canoe through the wilderness, clear to Castine, to find a priest who could marry them.

One of our own church women tells me that her grandmother, for whom she is named, was the milliner who made the mourning bonnet for Abraham Lincoln's widow. If that early Jenny had the conscience and skill of her namesake, it must have been a beautifully made bonnet. Our Jennie's conscience would not let her do anything the least bit carelessly and I have a beautifully embroidered "chair set" she made for me to bear out my statement. Maine ought to be a natural place for Methodists, with their doctrine of "going on to perfection." The older generation, at least, and some of the present generation hold themselves to an uncompromising standard in everything they do; and Heaven itself will have to have a special "spring cleaning" if it is to satisfy some of those who come from around here.

It was Sunday morning, and I was wide awake at five-thirty. "This is silly," I told myself firmly. "You have a hard day ahead of you—now go back to sleep till seven." But sleep wouldn't come. I never had been more wide-awake. Usually on Sundays I would rise about seven and then have the hour from eight to nine, after I had finished breakfast, to go over the sermon and spend the time in prayer and meditation. So on this Sunday morning I said, "Well, why not go over the sermon now, in bed, and if I fall asleep over it it won't do any harm." I went downstairs to get it, crawled back into bed, and went over it in my mind, praying for the various people in my churches and asking God to use the services of the day for His glory and His purpose in these lives. At six-thirty I was even more wakeful, so I got up, feeling very strange about such a beginning to the day. At seven, as I had just finished dressing and was making a cup of coffee, the telephone rang. One of the neighbors had shot himself!

We never knew why. No one had realized that he was brooding over a marriage that had gone on the rocks several years before. As far as anyone knew, his business affairs were in order and he had no known disease. But here was the tragic fact. I dashed down to the house, wondering at the strange dear Providence that had got me ready to be free to help, with no anxiety about the church services to follow. I was able to be with the family, a housekeeper and a young son, who had slept in the same room with his father and had been awakened by the shot, and who was in deep shock. I telephoned the Naval Base where the older son was stationed and talked to the Commander, who agreed to break the news as gently as he could and send the boy home, and I stayed with them until time for church. The services must have had a deeper note that day—of wonder at the God who cared to see that I was awake and ready to help, yet whose caring for his distressed child could not prevent the tragedy. Where had we failed, all of us who had been unaware of mental pain under the calm, seemingly normal surface of daily life?

The following Friday the older son planned to return to the Naval Base. I stopped in to say goodbye. Most of that week I had been with the family in one way or another. When I arrived at the little apartment I found that he had received an extension of his leave and was going with his wife and young baby to spend a few days with her family in central New Brunswick. As we talked about the journey

I found it would take twenty-four hours at least, involving four changes of train with long stopovers. After all they had been through it seemed like too much to undertake with a four-month-old baby, and the resultant problems of feeding, changing, and all the rest. I had never been to Canada, and this looked like a golden opportunity. The housekeeper had never been there, either, and she too needed the change. So we started out at one in the afternoon. We reached the border about sunset and pressed on to St. John, where at eight o'clock we found a restaurant open. Nearby was a little store and newsstand where coffee and hamburgers were sold. I took the baby's bottle in and asked the clerk if he would mind warming it for me. Obviously he thought I was the grandmother and with a proud smile replied, "I know just how to do it, ma'am, I have one of my own." As the bottle was warming he cooked me a hamburger, and with the bottle in one hand and the hamburger in the other I went back to the car and fed the baby while my passengers went into the restaurant for their supper.

Those New Brunswick roads were dark as we worked our way upstate through miles of wilderness. I wondered if we might meet a moose, and recalled that I had been told that a bull moose would charge a moving car. The rule is to stop the car, turn off the lights and motor, and sit tight. But we saw no moose, nor even a deer that night. A raccoon or two, several porcupine, and an occasional skunk were the only signs of wild life. After a while we came to the edge of a large lake. "How in the world did we get here?" the little wife exclaimed. "I must have told you wrong at the last fork."

It was a long way back to that last fork, I thought with dismay.

"We ought to be the other side of this lake," she said.

"I know where we are, all right, and it's at least twenty-five miles out of the way!"

It was past midnight then, but back we went and eventually found the right turning. At three in the morning we drove up to her house!

The warm hospitality of the family, awakened at that unearthly hour, was remarkable. They wanted to give us food, and the bowl of hot tomato soup was good, but sleep was what we needed most. At three-thirty we tumbled into bed for three hours' sleep, for it was already Saturday and Sunday was close at hand. A six-hundred-mile trip with no sleep is not the best preparation for a day's preaching, but somehow God took care of that too, as he had the previous Sunday. The energy held up and the sermon "went over."

On that trip, as we had crossed the border, the customs officer had asked about cameras and field glasses. There was no camera with us but there were field glasses—the prized possession of young Chandler. Because we had no permit to take them into Canada, we left them at the customs office, and the officer in charge said they had to be taken out in the same car which brought them in. Since Chandler was not returning with me but was planning to return by train I had to pick them up and bring them back, and so I had the use of them for many months, until he had another leave and came back to see his younger brother. Watching birds had always been such a joy that the use of these glasses was wonderful recompense for the wear and tear of the trip and I increased my bird list amazingly. Suddenly I began to know the water birds. They had usually been too far away and too much confused by glare for positive identification without the help of binoculars. Now with the glasses I found grebes, all sorts of ducks, and many kinds of sandpipers frequenting our bay and grassy shores. In fact it was such fun to have the glasses that I determined someday to have a pair of my own—and the next year, when I finally finished the study course and received my ordination as an Elder of the Methodist Church, I bought a pair. For I knew that if my dear Chris had been there he would have bought some sort of present to mark the occasion and I felt that this was the appropriate thing to do. The glasses were of Japanese make, excellent both in field of vision and clarity, and from then on it was not uncommon for the trip to the post office to take an hour instead of fifteen minutes, while the neighbors saw the "parson" peering into the woods with her binoculars. I thought, occasionally, that if I were as concerned with finding a new convert as I was in spotting a new bird, the Kingdom of God would prosper faster. Yet reverence for the ways of God with little birds certainly made me more aware of His care for His human children. Perhaps if one is to know what Jesus meant when he said, "Ye are of more value than many sparrows," he has to learn to really value and appreciate the sparrows first. Anyhow, that's my alibi!

As the family of churches increased, and as I became acquainted with more and more families in each of my towns and in the neighboring towns where I had no church work, remembering names became more and more of a problem. It was bad enough when I went to each of my own communities. Everybody knew me for I was the only stranger, but there were some six hundred of them to learn all at once. As soon as I had one family fairly well organized in my mind I would meet some of their relatives in another town. Everybody seemed related to everybody else. And when I

went to Ellsworth to shop it was just hopeless. At least when
they were at home I had things to go by; after all, people in
Gouldsboro are likely to be Tracys or Youngs, and in Sullivan
to be Gordons, Haveys, or Robertsons, but in Ellsworth it
was anybody's guess. Many embarrassing situations arose out
of my inability to remember who was who, but the worst
of all was one day in the First National Store. I saw someone approach me with a beaming smile, and while my mind
was frantically saying, Who in the world are you? Which
of my towns do you come from? my voice was saying, "Hello
—I'm so glad to see you, how are you?" trying to make up
in warmth of tone what I lacked in knowledge.

"I'm much better," came the reply.

If I had only said, "That's good—" and left it alone! But
feeling very much on the defensive I said, "Oh, I didn't
know you'd been sick."

Her jaw dropped and her eyes widened as she said, "But
you came to see me the day before I went to the hospital!"

There wasn't any way out of that one. Now I ask out-
right, "Won't you tell me who you are?" But to this day
I don't know the identity of the lady in the First National.
Covered with confusion, I apologized for not remembering,
she observed that I must have a great deal on my mind,
and I went off wondering if I had any mind to have anything on.

A delightful new family came to live in our town about
this time. Before long we saw letters spelling out POTTERY
KILN and WORKSHOP on the side of one of our old houses.
The potter, tall, dark, with a quiet smile and a friendly
manner behind his deep eyes, was from the Isle of Jersey.
Bit by bit his story became known. His family had always

lived there, and when the Germans occupied the island during the war they were evacuated. Denis, however, returned for some necessary things, was caught, and only after fifteen months, grim months about which he says nothing, managed to escape by rowing three days and nights in an open boat to England. How he had endured the trip without food or water no one knows, but at last he made it, nearly dead of exhaustion. From England he came to Canada for training in the R.A.F. and while in training met and fell in love with a girl from Montreal whose father was born and brought up here in Sullivan. So after the war they decided to come here and make a living, if they could, on the old place.

Denis is an artist and craftsman of a very high order. Originally interested in wood carving, he turned to pottery and was delighted to find a vein of suitable clay right here in this locality. With his own hands he worked for months to convert the old barn into a workshop and build a kiln. It was desperately hard to build a kiln that would stand the terrific heat that fine pottery requires, but after two years of real struggle the work was done and the shop ready to do business. Such beautiful things he makes—they have reality and strength and art. All the fierce struggle of his spirit through the days of danger and of effort to establish himself have built a rugged fineness of character that is expressed through his sensitive fingers. He makes his own glazes and they are beautiful beyond words. The whole community was glad when he received recognition by being elected to membership in the Boston Society of Arts and Crafts. For many years our neighboring town of Hancock, just across the bridge, has been a center of great music, built around the conductor Pierre Monteux and his summer school of conducting. Musicians of top rank come here to study and compose. Now we also have this beautiful pottery to enrich our lives.

Not far from the pottery was a little red-shingled cottage. It had two rooms downstairs, a bedroom upstairs, and a shed. Here lived another Englishman and his wife. Whenever I stopped to call I was served a cup of strong English tea and entertained with warm and friendly conversation. The man had been engineer of a steam vessel that traveled the coast in older days. One morning the phone rang and the operator told me he had had a shock. "I thought you ought to know," she said. I thanked her and hurried down to the house.

The devoted wife had not left his bedside for two days except to get an occasional cup of tea. Her husband's face was very red, his breathing fast and shallow, but he knew me and was glad to see me. I spoke to him quietly and presently I realized that he was desperately trying to tell me something. His wife and I listened carefully and found that he was trying to say he wanted to be baptized. She said to me, " 'E's often talked about it, but 'e kept putting it off." He was a man of fine principle and a kind heart, but he didn't want to leave this world unbaptized, and I felt that his very anxiety about it was probably no help to his blood pressure.

His wife had told me when I first arrived that the doctor wanted him to have an ice pack, but of course they had no ice. So home I went to get my ice pack and fill it with cubes from my refrigerator, to pick up a can of corned beef hash from my pantry shelf, along with some other things I thought she might enjoy. And with these in one hand and the silver baptismal font and my service book in the other, I made my way back to the little house. First aid and food and religion all mixed up together! It is a good symbol of the life of a country pastor.

His color was better now, not nearly so red. He had rested in my absence, content at the thought of baptism, and was entirely clear in his mind and much more clear in his speech as we had the simple little service for them both. Two days later he left this life—and when I went again to see the wife she kept saying, with the tears raining down her cheeks, "I'm so glad he took the step, I'm so glad he took the step." And I was glad too.

Another of our older men "took the step" on a certain Sunday. Luther is blind, but sees with the eyes of the heart —more sensitive than any eye can be. I had often gone to his house and marveled at his independence in finding his way around the dooryard and out into the garden. He had a wonderful garden—his potatoes were famous, and his raspberries. They were desperately poor as far as things are concerned but wonderfully rich in spirit. In fact, I found myself hesitating to call there often, for they always insisted on my taking home apples, or berries or potatoes. Whatever they had they shared with the pastor. And every bit of the work of raising these things had been done by blind Luther and his thin hard-working wife. Moreover, they had with them a granddaughter whose abnormality made it necessary for her to be away from her other brothers and sisters. This child of twenty years or more could not talk plainly but made grunting animal-like cries of pleasure or pain. She had to be watched carefully, but her grandmother took care of her with loving devotion and the sweet patient smile and gentle voice of the grandfather made one forget that he could not see.

On this particular Sunday, then, just as the service started

I looked up to see Luther coming in to church, led by one of his grandsons. I had already gone up into the pulpit, so there was no opportunity for conversation. It was a day when some young people were to be baptized. As the service progressed I noticed the emotion evident on the face of this stalwart man. When we came to the point of calling the candidates forward, he stood up straight and tall in his place and in a firm mellow voice said, "Is it too late for me to come too?"

I assured him that it was not and went down the aisle to take his hand and bring him forward. I am sure no baptism was ever quite so impressive in that little church. We all knew the years of courage and sincerity that had built strength and gentleness into that voice, and character and appreciation into that life. On one occasion he had said to me, "Nobody couldn't live here and watch these tides day in and day out and not know Somebody was in charge of things." Now as he answered the solemn question great tears ran down his lined face and across his soft beard—but his head was lifted up and it almost seemed as if light shone in those sightless eyes. There was lilt and depth in his voice as he took the vows and I felt he was seeing a Glory and feeling a Companionship of the One who had touched many a blind eye and brought sight again.

NINE

PREPARING SERMONS IS A BIT LIKE WRITING MUSIC. AT LEAST I think it must be. I am no musician, but I enjoy great symphonies and I know that a symphony is built around certain themes that recur in the different voices of the various instruments, sometimes in different keys or with varying rhythms, but all working out in a pattern of beauty. In any art form there has to be rhythm, line, and color. These things have their parallel in preaching. It has often seemed to me that the "line" in painting or sculpture, like the melodic line in music, had its counterpart in a sermon as the truth seen and expressed was related to daily living and individual experience. In the same way the harmonies of music, the deep underlying chords and rhythms, or the texture in painting, could be compared to the way a sermon is firmly grounded in Scripture. And the color and grace and individuality in these other forms of art are paralleled by the illustrations that make a sermon live and sparkle and stay in the heart. Anyhow, sermons must have these two anchors—the anchor

in the individual soul and the anchor in Scripture and the spiritual experience of the race; and they must have the "rest spots"—the illustrations, the "windows" that let in fresh air and sunlight and keep the whole from being stuffy. And of course they must have, above all else, the sense of imperative and conviction—that burning sense that this is the tremendous truth of God as far as we are given to see it.

From the beginning I enjoyed studying and preparing sermons. It was fun to read a familiar passage of Scripture and have it suddenly spring to life, familiar words, words one had always known, but suddenly become glowing. Sometimes it seemed as if I must call up friends in faraway places to share with them some new discovery. Yet I knew that probably to them the words had always carried this same exciting meaning—and that if they had not yet made the discovery, my telling them wouldn't make much difference, for this deeper knowing is a very individual matter, an adventure of spirit that each of us must make for himself. Yet it was my business to share it as vividly as I could.

The trouble was the fight for time. The pastoral work was increasing. The more families I got to know, the more people came to trust me, the heavier the load and the less time for study, meditation, and creative work. I suppose many a layman thinks of a pastor as one who has little to do between Sundays but sit in his study and meditate—read helpful books and pray. That certainly is far from the true picture as I have come to know it. What little time I could get for real study was further trespassed upon by glaring needs in the house; floors that had to be swept or washed, windows that had become so smoky they cried out to be washed, some ironing and mending—although I did as little as I possibly could. Yes, the trouble was that having chosen

to be the minister I also had to be "her wife." And then
there was the study course, twelve books a year to be mastered, with papers to be written endlessly for almost every
chapter of every book had its assigned written work. On six
books a year examinations were given—and these six books
were naturally enough the harder, heavier, and more important ones.

Often I wondered what was the matter with the men
who made up the study assignments. In the first place, like
all professors, they seemed to think that theirs was the only
course to be studied and that there was no limit to the time
one had for their subject. And then the assignments of subjects for hypothetical sermons! I suppose somebody had a
vague notion that the sermons written for the study course
would be useful in the pastorate, but I found myself alter-
nately disgusted or highly amused at the thought of preaching to my people on some of these subjects. Many of the
assignments were sensible and good in the way they opened
up avenues of thought, but there were some that induced
only mild hysterics as I thought of my self trying to preach
on such topics. I think the prize one was "Outline and write
out in full a talk which you would make to the men of your
church at some informal meeting on 'The Common Faults
and Noble Virtues of Men.'" The reference was to the stories
of Joab, Abner, and David. Somehow I couldn't picture
myself haranguing my fine neighbors on the common faults
and noble virtues of men! They knew their faults all too
well; certainly if I had tried to point out their noble virtues
I would have been under suspicion as a scheming woman.
Another gem was an assignment to write a sermon on "Playing with Fire." Now I am sure that much must be said from
the pulpit on such subjects, but somehow the attempt to do

it as a written assignment, and not out of a compelling sense
of responsibility for the social situation before one, made it
slightly ridiculous—especially when it is grounded in some
of the very frank passages in the book of Proverbs. And it
seemed rather far removed from the daily scene, to write
a paper comparing the characters of Jacob, Joseph, and
Potiphar.

But out of such efforts came two great goods. First, the
detailed study of the entire Bible, not only the parts one
had known more or less well always, but the parts that had
been neglected. Reading these so carefully and thoughtfully
turned up many new insights. Second, the habit of studying
and writing, the discipline of regular work. Five years of
such study, with deadlines to meet each year, and a certain
amount of work that had to be got through, was a very good
beginning for a pastor who found it easy to follow the call
of the wild, or the call of the parish, or the call of her own
heart, and so tended to put off these matters of study and
just plain work.

Some of the books were truly great and my life is richer
for having had to study them. Brightman's *An Introduction
to Philosophy*, Fosdick's *Guide to Understanding the Bible*,
Nagler's *Church History*, Branscomb's *The Teachings of
Jesus*, Bennett's *Social Salvation*, and others of that sort
were solid meat. Along with these I read some other books
not required, but extremely helpful—Du Noüy's *Human
Destiny*, Trueblood's *Common Ventures of Life*, Rufus
Jones, Nels Ferré, Toynbee's *Study of History*, Reinhold
Niebuhr. It was a land of giants among whom I was living
and the mind-stretching felt good. It had been many years
since I had done serious hard study. But of course there
were other books to explain techniques of the pastor's job

that were very boring and slow going, such uninspired titles as *Achieving Results in Church Finance, The Minister Teaches Religion, The Church in Our Town*. Such books have their uses, of course—they are the "know-how" books of the craft, but as in secular education the danger is that we shall substitute facility in "know how" for philosophy of "know why." It is most tragic of all in religion when we try to substitute "know how" for "know Who," for Christian faith and experience is first of all a deep friendship, a love affair between a man and Christ.

As I look over the student handbook now I am glad I took the course when I did. For it seems to me that it has less solid meat in it now. It has become a bit shorter and easier, and has possibly lost something of the great mind-stretching disciplines brought by those stiffer books required five and six years ago. Most helpful of all, perhaps, was a thin little book of the first year about country parishes called *Highland Shepherds*. When I find myself feeling uninspired I turn it over and over again. It never fails to reawaken the sense of the High Calling.

Out of the combination of the study course and the necessity for having real sermons that applied to real situations, not hypothetical ones to satisfy an examiner, I found out certain things about preaching. One of them is that a sermon is not a logical discourse; after all, people do not concentrate for even twenty-minute stretches with unbroken attention. Rather it is weaving, more or less skillfully, as the case may be, a pattern of thought, with now one color, now another—a phrase here, an illustration there, an earnest exhortation, perhaps—a lilting assurance of faith. And I discovered too that a preacher doesn't make the sermon. The whole experience of worship in church is created by the

Holy Spirit moving into the invisible but real response and rapport between the preacher and the people. Their responsiveness is just as vital a part as the preacher's preparation— but how few congregations know it! Sometimes it seems as if one wandering attention is tearing a hole in that invisible fabric faster than it can be created. And this seems to be especially true during the pastoral prayer. One wandering distraction can do such disastrous things in destroying or lessening the reality of prayer, whereas the deep united caring of all the people does so much to build it.

On occasion, not often, when the whole community is anxious about a sick member or sympathetic toward a family going through a hard experience, I have in the church service prayed for certain people by name. It is always interesting to feel how the depth of prayer increases at that moment. The silence takes on a deeper quality, wandering thoughts have come back, the group is knit together in common concern. If the people in the pews only understood this, they would not commit the blasphemy of wandering attention during prayer, nor inattention and distraction when the Scripture is being read or the sermon delivered. They would worship God in spirit and in truth throughout every part of the Service for through this tiny group the Lord God waits for His church to be built in this place.

Occasionally sermons came almost as if by dictation. That is a wonderful experience. My fingers could hardly hit the typewriter keys as fast as words and ideas unfolded. More often though, it was hard work. "Blood, sweat and tears" went into their manufacture. The Bible speaks occasionally of the whole creation "groaning and travailling together" and sometimes it seemed as if a week in a preacher's life was like that most of all. I know why they speak of sermons being "delivered." Many a time I have come up to the end of the week feeling that I was being delivered of a sermon, and the pregnancy of thought and feeling had been heavy almost beyond endurance. After agonizing and laboring over a sermon that way it was heartbreaking to have a congregation of perhaps only eight or twelve or twenty, and know that the others could have shared in the worship and contributed their own faith to its making if they had only realized how much they were needed.

I have been blessed—or cursed—with superacute hearing. Occasionally in church a worshiper will absent-mindedly wind his wrist watch during the prayer. In one church my organist used to do it, or in summer, when wearing a short-sleeved dress, would scratch her elbow. She was a nervous person and I knew it wasn't deliberate disturbance but it indicated that she wasn't deeply in the mood of prayer, and somehow after such sounds I found my prayer coming up to the surface and to a quick close. The wonderful depth of Communion had been broken. In one service a man did quite a complete job on his fingernails in the back pew during the Scripture reading. He didn't realize, of course, that the pulpit was enough higher so that I could see what was going on. It was hard to ignore such breaks in the fabric of worship and I would come to the close of the service quite exhausted from the nervous energy expended to catch and hold attention. One small group whose service was in the afternoon had two elderly ladies who were evidently used to afternoon naps. I knew that at their age it was not to be expected that they would keep alert and interested. I am sure that if I had been in their places, as frail as they were, I wouldn't have made the effort they made to attend church at all. But every once in a while when I saw their eyes glaze

over and their heads nod, I would have an insane tempta-
tion to recite "Twinkle, Twinkle, Little Star" right in the
middle of the sermon to see if they would take notice and
wake up, or, for that matter, if anyone would.

One Sunday this acute hearing of mine was very useful.
A strange lad came in to the service. I knew who he was,
a boy about twelve who had recently come to board with
one of our families. He sat down in the back pew, near the
door—the pew where I usually laid my coat and pocketbook.
As I preached I noticed the intentness of his gaze; he fixed
me with his eyes, in a way most unusual for a youngster. I
saw his arm stretch out inch by inch toward the corner where
my pocketbook was. I could not actually see the purse, the
back of the pew before him was too high, but the combination of that slow, stealthily moving arm and his gaze fixed
on my face told me what was happening. The catch on the
purse moved very easily so I heard no click, but I did see
the arm come back and heard the faint crinkle of a dollar bill
as his hand slid into his pocket, a crinkle that is different
from the soft rustle of other paper. After a while his hand
moved from the pants pocket to the shirt pocket, and again
I heard the crackle of money.

After church I said goodbye to him as cordially as to the
others, said I was glad he had come and hoped he would
come again. I made no effort to examine my pocketbook until
I had left the church and was out of sight. I didn't propose
to have anyone start gossip or condemnation. When I got
out of sight I stopped the car and looked. I knew that the
seven dollars given to me in the previous church had been
hastily tucked behind the mirror as I left the church, rather
than being put in the inner zipper pocket. I counted the bills
there behind the mirror and there were six of them.

After the day's work was done I went around to the boy's house and asked to speak to him. The foster parents were a bit on guard. "Is anything wrong?" the father asked.

I replied, "I just want to see him for a minute." So the lad came downstairs and we talked about church and Sunday School until the parents left the room for something. Then I said, "You're lonely, aren't you?"

His eyes filled with sudden tears. Before he had a chance to say anything I followed it with "What were you going to do with that dollar?"

"Oh, I'll give it back," he said quickly.

"Yes," I said, "I knew you would. But that's how I knew you were lonely. Happy boys don't do those things—so I wondered if I could help."

We talked a minute or two. I assured him that this was just between us. "You won't tell my folks?" he asked, not quite sure.

"No," I said, "this is between us and God. He knows about how you feel and He understands when a fellow feels lonely and does some silly babyish thing. And he forgives us always, if we really want Him to, and gives us another chance—"

Quickly the lad excused himself, ran up to his room, and came down, a Sunday School paper in one hand, the dollar bill in the other. As he asked me a question, obviously for his foster mother's benefit, he slipped the dollar bill into my hand.

A few weeks later I learned that the agency responsible for his care had moved him to a new foster home in another town. I hope he is happier there and I think he may be, for not long ago he saw me when I went in to do some shopping in Ellsworth and ran across the street to catch up with me and walk downtown. My heart was singing that he felt

confident of my friendship and wasn't ashamed to meet me
easily. I wondered if God doesn't want us to come back to
Him as naturally after He has confronted us with our sins
of pride and pretense—so much more serious, really, than a
lonely boy's sin against property.

At last the study course was completed—the final paper
had been turned in, the last examination taken and passed.
It seemed strange to think that there was no more of that
pressure. Conference was coming, and with it my ordination
service. Over and over again I read the service, the solemn
questions about one's intention to devote oneself wholly to
the work of the ministry and to "fashion your own lives and
those of your family according to the teachings of Christ."
Above all other sentences in the charge I felt the ones that
said, "They unto whom you are to minister are the sheep of
Christ for whom He gave His life. And if it shall happen the
church or any member thereof do take hurt or hindrance by
reason of your negligence, you know the greatness of the
fault." Truly this was a responsibility to be undertaken only
at the inescapable call of Christ, only under the compelling
pressure of the Holy Spirit. Conference Sunday was just
ahead. I pictured the service as I had seen it performed for
others: the group of earnest young men standing before the
Bishop to receive the solemn charge, their kneeling figures
as the hands of the Bishop, the Elders, and District Superintendents were laid on their heads in the act of ordination.
I pictured it over and over again in my mind and felt that
this supreme experience, for which I had been preparing so
long, would be a wonderful moment.

And then, the Sunday before I was to go to Conference,
one of our boys, a fine lad of fifteen—whose eyes had been

full of feeling throughout the sermon—waited for me after church, and with some effort said, "Mrs. Henrichsen, could I join the church next Sunday?"

There was a moment of panic—the next Sunday was Conference Sunday. I was to be ordained in a city about one hundred and fifty miles away! And then I realized what was in that boy's face, what he had been feeling and working through. The next Sunday was not only the date for my ordination, it was Mother's Day. This boy's decision was his Mother's Day gift to his mother. It meant everything to him and I said, "Of course you may. It will be wonderful for us all to have you."

When I got to Conference I looked up the Bishop and explained the situation, saying to him, "Of course I'd like my ordination this year—and I'm ready for it, but when a boy comes to you with that sort of experience and feeling you don't say to him, 'No, you'll have to wait a week.'"

The Bishop agreed that it was too important for the boy to be put off. I said I would be willing to wait for another year if necessary, but if it could be done at some other time than Sunday I would like to have it then, so that I could return home an ordained minister for my people, and ready for that Mother's Day in my own church. We looked over the program together, found a space at five o'clock on Friday, just after the close of the afternoon business session, and so it was, that instead of joining the class of young men on Sunday afternoon, I was ordained all by myself.

But it couldn't have been more meaningful for me. The faith of those wonderful ministers and laymen who were entrusting me with this part of the church work, the call of Christ, the sense that His power was there for my need! And when at the close of the service we sang a hymn whose verses

included the words, "They watch for souls for whom the
Lord did heavenly bliss forego, for souls that must forever
live in rapture or in woe," with the last verse, "May they in
Jesus whom they preach their own redeemer see, and watch
Thou daily o'er their souls, that they may watch for Thee,"
I found my eyes brimming over. As the men and women who
were to be my brothers and sisters of the ministry came up
to congratulate me afterward the pent-up feeling suddenly
broke in a great wave of love for what these dear people
stood for and the work we were called to do together.

Most curious of all, perhaps, was the depth of the experience in its utter quietness. When I was married I had felt
that that would be life's highest moment until the moment of
graduation out of this life into the heavenly kingdom. But
that day of ordination was an even deeper happiness and a
higher moment than my wedding day had been. And perhaps because it meant all that for me, the next Sunday was
the high point it should have been for a fourteen-year-old
boy who was paying his mother the finest tribute and giving
her the greatest gift his boyish soul knew how to give.

I long to have the weddings I perform be high and holy
moments in the lives of those who come, but it is not always
easy to make them supremely beautiful. It depends, of course,
on what the bride and groom bring to their wedding in the
way of spiritual understanding. And many a country minister has weddings which are not planned for much ahead
of the date.

One man who came to see me brought his young son with
him. The wedding for which he wanted to plan was a second
marriage and he spent most of the time telling me about the
sins and failures of the first wife. I felt this wasn't the most

helpful sort of conversation for the six year old to be taking in, so to break the trend of thought I said to the little boy, "I have a nice picture of Jesus in my study—wouldn't you like to see it?"

They came in together, the father with his weather-lined face, and the little boy. Then gently the man took off his cap, which he had not thought to remove before, and he said to his little son, "How would you like to have the power that Man had? I bet you he could cut twenty-six cords of wood a minute!"

An unusual but nonetheless sincere recognition of the wonder-working power of Divinity!

There was another wedding, crowded into an already over-crowded Sunday, which was to be held at a lakeside cottage. It was a question as to whether I could make connections and be there at four o'clock. The rustic cottage had been made attractive with evergreens and candles and it was a lovely setting for a wedding. But in my haste, arriving at the last minute when everything was ready, I hadn't thought to ask whether it was to be a double-ring or single-ring ceremony. When we had finished, the bride and groom embraced each other and were receiving the congratulations of the guests when the maid of honor came up to me and said wonder-ingly, as she held up the other ring, "What do I do with this?"

So we called them back and had the bride slip the ring on the groom's finger, with an extempore prayer in the middle of all the festivity! Now I find out first which service is to be used.

The books in the study course had had much to say about "marriage counseling." Surely it is a good idea. Ministers have an obligation to talk through this wonderful experience with the couple they are to marry. But in the country it just isn't possible to achieve the ideal of two or three interviews before a wedding, nor is it always necessary.

One afternoon my telephone rang and a crusty voice said, "Mrs. Henrichsen, can you come up here at seven o'clock tonight?" I recognized the voice as belonging to one of the older men of the town—a man who had for years owned a quarry and was used to having his own way. His tone was more command than question.

"No," I said, "I'm afraid I can't. I have promised to be in Ashville tonight just at seven."

"You can't eh?"—in a tone of great surprise—then, "Well, what time could you come?"

"I could come at six or at eight," I said, "but not at seven."

"Well, I guess six o'clock would be all right." And he hung up. He had not given his name, assuming that I knew who he was, and had made no mention of the reason for the appointment.

For a moment I thought he wanted to make his peace with God in my presence. He had been seriously ill a few months before and I thought perhaps he had decided he ought to talk some things over with his minister. Or possibly he wants me to witness the making of a will, I thought to myself. Then the thought came, No, he wouldn't set a definite hour for those things. I bet he wants to marry his housekeeper.

His housekeeper had been faithfulness itself in the years since his wife's death, and by marrying her, I supposed, he could settle his property on her more easily in the event of his death. So, acting on my hunch, I took my service book and robe when I went out at six o'clock, but I left them in the car. I went in through the kitchen door, always the casual entrance into a country home, and there they were. He had on a necktie, the first time I had ever seen him so formally

dressed. She was in her best maroon silk, and they were
sitting at the kitchen table blushing like eighteen year olds,
though they were both well past seventy. I was wicked
enough to make conversation for a few minutes, ignoring
their splendor, and then asked innocently, "And what can I
do for you?"

He fairly exploded in his eagerness, "You might marry us."
So I did.

But some of our weddings were so carefully planned, so
lovingly carried out, so really beautiful! I think I'll never
forget the one in one of our smallest churches. There were
only eight people there, the groom's mother and brother, the
organist whom I had secured, and two guests of my own who
were visiting me at the time. The bride was a beautiful girl,
a nurse from one of our city hospitals. Her own family lived
in central New York State, and as her mother was ill they
were unable to be present. She knew no one in our community except the groom and his family but she had always
wanted a church wedding. I stood waiting with the groom
and his brother in front of a great banking of apple blossoms
on the altar, looking out through the doorway to the sparkling sea until she appeared in shining white satin, as beautiful and radiant as any bride entering a great cathedral.
The groom had expected her to be wearing a travelling suit
and when he saw her his face lit up as if a great searchlight
had been suddenly turned on.

Another lovely church wedding was made more beautiful
by some tall wrought-iron nine-branched candlesticks which
we borrowed from a summer friend. But just before the
service started the groom, waiting with me and the best
man in the church vestry, realized the candles had not been

lighted. In the pouring rain his best man had to go out to the church doors to remind the ushers of their duty, while I had all I could do to keep the groom from flying into a rage of disappointment.

One night I came in after a long Sunday. There had been the usual six services and a funeral besides, and then I had made a call after church. It had been a very pleasant place in which to relax at the end of the day, so I had not hurried. As I drove up to the house about ten-thirty, I saw a car. A grieved voice said, "We've been waiting for you since seven o'clock."

"If I had only known you were coming," I said. I recognized them as a couple who had been "going together" for some time. "Well, come in—"

"Oh, we've got to go home and dress," they said. "We just waited to see if you would still do it tonight!"

It was after eleven when they came back, the middle-aged bride and groom, who after years of courtship decided they couldn't wait another day! As the bride took corsages out of the cellophane wrappings for herself and her attendant, she also took two white carnations out of another package and pinned them in the buttonholes of the groom and the best man. The best man's comment as he sniffed ecstatically was, "It stinks pretty!"

And there was a wedding I was called to perform in another town. It was being held at the home of the bride. About the time we were ready to begin, nearly an hour late because of one contingency after another, somebody asked, "Has anybody fed the lamb?"

In the excitement of the preparations the lamb in the barn had been forgotten, so again proceedings were held up until the lamb's formula had been mixed and duly administered. On that occasion, in order to bring the assembled guests and myself back to a sense of the sacredness of the occasion, I read the great hymn of love from the thirteenth chapter of First Corinthians before beginning the service. I needed it to steady myself, quite apart from the effect I hoped it would have on the guests.

But whether the couple are young or old, the ceremony carefully planned and carried out with white veils, music, and candlelight or performed in the parsonage parlor, whether with many guests or just the two required witnesses, there is something forever reverent and lovely about this service which unites two people as "husband and wife together." I am always glad to call to their attention the fact that in our form of service it is after they are so pronounced that we repeat the Lord's Prayer. Thus their first spoken words as husband and wife are the age-old words of dependence on God, submission to His will, the prayer to Him for daily bread, for the coming of His kingdom, and the realization of His power and glory forever. "And having started your life together that way," I usually say, "you need never feel shy about praying aloud together about your deepest needs—for prayer is already the very foundation of your married life. You have begun there."

TEN

TWO YEARS AND A HALF HAD GONE BY, AND HOW QUICKLY, since the day when I had come to this lovely countryside. I was already feeling really established, both in the parsonage and church work and in the life of the communities, and I did not see how anyone could have a fuller life. Every day had more to do in it than one could possibly manage. Then one day the telephone rang. It was a family in Franklin, the town where "nothing could be done" to reopen the church. The voice at the other end of the wire asked if I could come over to a meeting.

I went and found there a group of women, all friendly, quite beaming, in fact. Without further preliminary they said, "We want to reopen the church. There are thirty families pledged to support it and the only question is: Can you come to us—and what time?"

The only time I had free on my already overbusy Sunday was one o'clock in the afternoon—Sunday dinner hour the

country over. I wanted so much to do it, but as I explained my time schedule, I felt sure they would find that a stumbling block. Not at all! I had reckoned without knowing how real was their enthusiasm. "If that's the time you have, that's the time we'll come," they said. And they did and still do. In two weeks we were ready to hold our first service. The church was well filled and it has been one of the warmest, most enthusiastic congregations ever since.

By the next year we were ready to organize a Sunday School. For Superintendent there was a little lady, exquisite in gray silk, with apple-blossom cheeks, twinkling blue eyes, and a dignified manner that made you know she had been a New England teacher of the old school most of her life. She was well over seventy but she was eager to help; the younger women felt they would like to teach under her, and her scholars, as she called the boys and girls, loved and respected her. For three years she was a devoted Superintendent—then she felt she must give the work to younger hands, but the Sunday School still carries the impress of her devoted, upright, and kindly spirit.

One of the things that gladdened my heart about this Franklin church was the way the men of the town responded to it. Almost without exception they took as much responsibility as their wives. The state senator, whose car carried license plate number one, for he was senior senator and chairman of the State Tax Commission, found time in his busy life to be there every week. Moreover, he said he needed church to keep his own sense of direction straight in the midst of the political pressures he had to face! The state inspector of water and sanitation for this area was not only one of the trustees, but came across the street early to build the fire and do the janitor work, and when church began, he stood behind the musty old chenille curtain and pumped the organ—a fine old golden-oak, two-manual reed affair with pedals. It has a mellow tone and we hope someday to put a motor on it so that our pumper may sit and worship with his family. These two men, assisted Mr. Abbott, a carpenter, and under the leadership of Mr. Nickerson, skilled in construction, rebuilt the foundations of the furnace, fixed the underpinning, and continue to see that the property is kept in good repair.

The women made choir robes of cherry-red poplin, with white collars and black ties, for a choir of twelve of the most attractive teen-agers I have ever seen. Such lovely girls they were, pretty, unspoiled, enthusiastic. Under the leadership of their Sunday School teacher they became a very important focal point in the life of the church.

We had an enthusiastic high school principal in the town who came with the young people to youth fellowship meetings. He was especially good at drawing out the thinking of the group. There were some fine boys who came to these meetings, mostly juniors and seniors, serious-minded lads, for they knew that in a year or two they would be seeing service on the battlefields of the world. When I went on vacation the following February, three of these young people led the worship service in their own church and in the other churches of the circuit. Before long there was a large intermediate fellowship organized under the leadership of Mrs. Nickerson. It brought all the young people, from the fourth grade up, to the church for social evenings once a week, and the tremendous devotion and energy that she and her co-workers put into the effort made the church the Friday night gathering place for the young. Then an adult Bible Study Class was organized for Thursday evenings in the homes of the members. This was the church where nothing could be done! Suddenly we had a church program needing far more time than I could give.

We had decided at that very first meeting that we would try hard not to proselyte, that we would do nothing to encourage people to leave the other church, and would try to reach only those who had no "church home" or affiliation.

Trying to be particularly careful in that direction led me into one amusing situation. There was an old couple who lived some distance from the church. I was told that the woman was paralyzed—had had a "shock." I said I'd go to call. The people who told me of her looked doubtful, and one said hesitatingly, "Well, I don't know what sort of reception you'll get. She's peculiar."

Assuring them I didn't mind and would be prepared for anything, I went to the house where an elderly collie dog met me at the door with a growl but at the same time with a wagging tail. I chose to believe the tail, and went up on the porch unhesitatingly. There were shuffling steps. Finally a little old man, very much bent with rheumatism, opened the door and stood aside to let me in. He spoke sharply to the dog, who slid behind the stove, keeping a watchful eye on me. I sat down in one of the straight chairs beside a cluttered table as I greeted the old man and asked about his wife. He explained that she had been sick for a long time. I spoke with some sympathy of the difficulties of looking after a sick woman and a house and he answered cheerfully and bravely, though obviously he too was in a good deal of pain. He poked up the fire and got another stick of wood, while I took stock of the unwashed milk bottles, the empty cans, the crumbs on the table, and the general clutter of the house. Wasn't there anyone who could come in and help? I wondered. Then he led me into the adjoining bedroom, where the sick woman lay in an untidy bed. "I'm the new Methodist minister," I said heartily.

"Yes, I know you are," was her grim reply. Her face was stern. There was no sign of friendliness. The dog, still watchful, had come out from behind the stove and crawled under the bed to keep an eye on this stranger. I like dogs and made some comment on what good company a dog was, and she responded to that remark.

Then I said, "I'm trying to get acquainted with the people here and I just didn't know which church you felt was yours. Does the other minister come to see you?"

"He came once," she replied. "He asked me if I wanted him to read the Bible. I told him 'No.' He asked me if I wanted him to pray. I told him 'No.' He took his hat and went. Never saw him again." And all this in an expressionless voice and without the faintest glimmer of a smile.

"Well," I answered, "sometimes we need the strength and help that the Bible and prayer can give us and sometimes perhaps what we need most is a good laugh. Maybe it was one of those days for you."

That took her off guard. That was a reply she hadn't expected and I felt that she relaxed a bit. The lines about her mouth were not quite so taut. We visited a little longer and I tried to tell her one or two things I thought she would be interested in about the neighborhood and the people she used to know. She whined that nobody came to see her now and she guessed they had forgotten all about her. Then, without a word about religion, the Bible, or prayer, I got up and left.

About ten days later I called again. This time the dog

didn't growl, in fact he let me pat him, the husband was definitely friendly, and Mrs. Gordon admitted she "didn't feel quite so bad." But before long she launched into a tirade against the town, the neighbors, and the hardness of life in general. I tried to keep my tone sympathetic but cheerful, and again made it purely a social call. She was much more relaxed, though still unsmiling. At the end of my third call after another ten days, as I stood up to go I took hold of her hand, bowed my head, and offered a short prayer—without having asked her anything about it or said what I was going to do. As I got to the door she called, "You'll come again soon, won't you?"

After that, a bit of the Bible and prayer came quite naturally and easily into every call, and plenty of jolly talk too, until the days came when she really smiled and stopped being sorry for herself. The next year when I was asked to conduct her funeral service, I felt that it was for a real friend whose new life would hold great unfolding joy as she was freed from the crippling of body and mind that had held her spirit bound so long.

This was the town where there was a blueberry freezing plant. From late July to mid-September blueberries dominated the thinking of the town. Every able-bodied person worked at the factory. The women sorted and picked over berries as they came to them on conveyor belts and the men unloaded the boxes of berries from trucks and freight cars, for we not only processed our local berries but brought them in from all over New England and Canada. The very floor of the building was stained blue from juice and mash, but the berries that were offered for sale were clean and beautiful. Blueberries are a perishable crop, and during the season the factory worked nights and Sundays as well as every other day, to the complete disruption of every town activity. The factory brought a forty-thousand-dollar payroll into town and gave employment not only to the factory workers but to growers and harvesters all over this end of the state. The hills which would be so gloriously scarlet a little later now had a lovely blue bloom, and everywhere the blueberry land was measured off in sections by twine—each picker had his own plot to work. At the edges of the road were winnowing machines, wooden hoppers into which the berries were poured, where rotating paddles worked up a breeze that blew away much of the leaf and chaff. From this hopper the berries were poured into boxes that were then taken to the factory. There are other packing plants, of course, but the Northeastern Packing Company is the principal packer of blueberries in the country and operates a canning plant at Columbia Falls, about forty miles away, and a packing plant in Vermont, as well as this one where the berries are deep-frozen.

The third year we took our courage in our hands and invited the District Conference of the church to hold its fall meeting here. It was something of a proposition for a little two-room church without running water to entertain one hundred and twenty-five or more visiting delegates, but only a few had to remain overnight. Our women are wonderful cooks and the two meals they served were a demonstration of their skill as well as of their spirit. It was the first time that a rural "Circuit church" in this area had tried to entertain the District Conference.

Water had been short that summer and it failed altogether the week the Conference was to take place. The blueberry factory was still in operation, though not with full crew, but in spite of various difficulties we had a good meeting and felt that we were established in the eyes of the Conference as a "going" church.

Meanwhile the other church in town had had a change of pastors. The new minister was a friendly young man with a charming wife and small baby. I called there soon after they arrived and found him most willing to co-operate and eager to help build a new spirit between the churches. And when on Thanksgiving morning we held a union service in the Methodist church, one which had been planned by a committee from each church working together, one in which each pastor took part equally, there was such a real spirit of Thanksgiving and rejoicing that we could hardly contain it. Church members who had moved to other towns came back for that morning. Forty people from each of the churches were there at nine-thirty on Thanksgiving morning, among them "Aunt Carrie," a dear little lady of ninety-three who wept with joy that she should have lived to see this day of a union service between the churches of her town. There may have been bigger and more impressive services in city churches that day, but there was certainly no more joy than shone in those eighty faces and rang out in those eighty voices as we sang together the fine old chorale, "Now Thank We All Our God."

In all the parish it had been an uphill job to get the people to want to sing the great hymns of the church. It was hard for me to realize that they didn't know and had never sung such hymns as "O Zion Haste," "A Mighty Fortress Is Our God," "The Spacious Firmament on High," "Once to Every Man and Nation," "Ten Thousand Times Ten Thousand," and were shy even about "O God, Our Help

in Ages Past," "The King of Love My Shepherd Is," and
"Beneath the Cross of Jesus." But how their voices would
ring out on "In my heart there rings a melody" and "Bring
then in, Bring them in, Bring them in from the fields of Sin,"
or "You may have the joy-bells ringing in your heart." My
own education was entirely lacking in hymns of this type.
I respected their enthusiasm and the fact that the Gospel
songs had for them the same associations that the others
had for me, yet how could they learn to love some of the
great hymns if they wouldn't even try them?

In Prospect Harbor we worked out a scheme by which
the congregation gathered for a fifteen-minute song service
before church began. I usually managed to get there for the
last part of it and so became familiar with some of their
favorites. Then, having sung hymns of their own choice,
they were willing to accept my selections for the service
and I learned which ones they liked, so that we could use
those, too. I drew the line, however, at one evidently written
for a railroad Y.M.C.A., or something of that sort, which
referred to heaven as "the Union Depot" and had a refrain,
"Keep your hand upon the throttle and your eye upon the
rail." "His Eye Is on the Sparrow" was another that I
avoided. While I knew it meant much to some of the older
people, I had watched too many sparrows through my binoculars to find it a worshipful hymn.

The best approach to the music problem was worked out
through the schools. A young woman who served as organist
at Sullivan had a great musical gift. Blessed with "absolute
pitch" and a fine tone quality, and trained in junior college
in piano, voice, and organ, she was able to respond to the
fine old hymns and to see their intrinsic beauty. Her husband worked for a summer family who appreciated her

musical gifts and subsidized a program of music teaching in the schools. By helping all the children in the school-rooms to learn good folk songs by rote, and by teaching them to read music at sight, she has greatly helped our musical standard and now we can call for many of the lovely hymns in the book without having people close their books in disgust.

One stormy day I went to the first service in the morning to find only one small boy and his father there. When it was apparent that no one else was coming the father suggested that we have no service, but somehow because that boy had come I didn't feel it would be right. So we had the regular service of worship leading up to the sermon, and I didn't try to preach but used the children's sermon. It had a message for the father as well as for his son. When it came to the hymns, I thought we'd better have something Sturgis knew, so I asked him to choose the hymn. To my utter amazement he chose one with a beautiful melody, the old German chorale "Liebster Jesu." I exclaimed, "Why Sturgis, I love that tune but I have never tried to have it here because no one knows it. How did you learn it?" And he replied, "You sang it once last summer." So we had, when summer people were there to help carry the lovely but unfamiliar melody. This boy had loved the beautiful old tune and remembered it, and so we sang it on that snowy morning, Sturgis, his father and I.

From time to time the musical abilities of our summer friends has added enormously to the beauty of our services. One year we had as summer visitor a man who had been organist for the Yale Divinity School and who had given at least one recital on the organ at Notre Dame Cathedral in

Paris. That summer he came to church regularly and from
our little reed organ brought music that was truly beautiful.
Following this, we had for several years a teacher from the
New England Conservatory of Music who was also secretary
of the Boston Bach Society. She was not well, and her getting up in time for a nine-thirty service all summer was a
real sacrifice. But how much she did for that little church!
Her splendid music added something to the service that
brought worshipers week after week. Somehow, to start the
day with God in a little one-room church in need of paint,
with the sparkling sea outside, the woods close behind, the
friendly group of year-round people and summer people
worshiping together through such lovely hymns, voluntaries,
and offertories as she played, was an experience of reality
that made all life more fine. And following her in that same
church we have had as organist for the last two years
Corinne LaComblé, soloist with the San Francisco and
Boston Symphony orchestras.

Mrs. LaComblé gave so much more than her very great
musical skill—she gave the most warmhearted enthusiasm
to the church. I used to tease her a bit, and brag about
her to others, because with even the simplest hymns she
wanted the numbers the day before, so that she might go
to the church and practice them. Her adoring husband was
as proud of his wife's contribution to the church as to the
concert stage, and as sincere in his own worship, giving
unstinted appreciation of every part of the service, from the
sermon to the decorous small boy who so seriously took up
the offering. How many times I have thought of my early
mental pictures of little "neglected, forlorn" churches! Somehow, this wonderful music given by great musicians along

with beauty and reality of their worship doesn't quite fit that pathetic picture. God still works His miracles of beauty and grace in His abundant providence.

In other churches there were generous gifts of special music, too. Dr. Isidore Freed of New York comes at least once each summer to the Sullivan church to play the organ, sometimes bringing with him the cellist Milton Forstadt, who has a summer home in the adjoining town, or violinists vacationing at the Monteux summer school of conducting just across the bridge. Sometimes Clara Rabinovitch or Ludwig Weiller, visiting friends in Ashville, would play for the services there. It was always thrilling to me to hear the singing in the Ashville church in summer, because the various members of the Schieffelin and Osborn families who summered there all attended church, all liked to sing, and knew good music. And from the smallest brown-eyed Osborn to great-grandfather Schieffelin the music would ring out—not only on "Throw Out the Life Line" and "Blessed Assurance" but also on "Praise to the Lord, the Almighty, the King of Creation," "Ein' Feste Burg," or the glorious hymn written from Schiller's "Ode to Joy" and set to the music of the Beethoven Ninth Symphony, or "Finlandia." And so, little by little, we were able to leave such things as "Life's Railway to Heaven" and "Out of the Ivory Palaces" and turn more often to those hymns of greater age and truer musical feeling.

Christmas music gave us a special opportunity for beauty of both song and symbol. In a very few years the candle-lighting service had become a custom and we were singing all the traditional carols. The children in the schools, under Mrs. Havey's direction, learned not only these but some of the more unusual ones—the Bohemian "Here Where the Oxen Kneel in Joy," the Polish carol "Infant Holy, Infant Lowly" and Christina Rossetti's "In the Bleak Mid-Winter." For two years we had the school bus take all the children from church to church, bringing these and other carols, giving us an augmented choir, and introducing some of these lovely things to churches which had no choirs at all.

One Christmas there was a program in a home, a little two-room house, scrubbed spick and span, where a fine young couple, childless themselves, had recently adopted a year-old baby. The young wife had held a Sunday School in her own kitchen for the neighborhood children because church was too far for them to walk. She had asked me to come and bring the Christmas story from the Bible. When I got there the tiny kitchen was almost completely filled. Back of the stove and along one side of the room were ten straight chairs. I have no doubt that she had borrowed from the entire neighborhood. On the other side of the stove were nine more chairs for the children. The house was spotless—the linoleum scrubbed, the wainscoting around the sink freshly painted. At the end of the sink was a small Christmas tree loaded with popcorn bags. Across the room, above the sink, was a single strand of tinsel from which hung many stars that she had cut from brown wrapping paper and crayoned in different colors. Below the sink, thumbtacked to the woodwork, was an ox, also cut from brown paper and crayoned. His horns were realistic and his eyes were a baleful green.

This was background scenery. For presently the program began. The nine children, singly, and in twos and threes, sang their Christmas songs and recited "pieces" they had learned. Then came the tableau. Two of the boys carried

in a large carton filled with hay and placed it in front of
the ox. Then the mother picked up her own baby boy, laid
him in the hay, covered him with a pink blanket. He
promptly put his thumb in his mouth and prepared to go
to sleep. The two oldest children came in, Joseph with a
shawl around his shoulders, Mary in a white nightgown
looped up with a scarf over her head. They took their places
at the head of the crib. Then three middle-sized boys came
in with scarves around their heads and shepherd staves in
their hands and knelt before the crib. Then the three smallest, with white angel wings pinned to their shoulders, came
and stood as the heavenly host. When one of them left the
angelic ranks to let the cat out, it didn't seem in the least
incongruous. After a few moments of reverent silence Mary
said, "Amen," and then they all sang "Silent Night." Reality
of worship doesn't depend on musicianship!

After the program the popcorn bags were distributed,
there was a present for every child, and a candy basket
provided by a neighbor, and we went out into the still night
air, grateful for the coolness after that hot little kitchen with
its blazing wood fire, feeling that here once again we had
touched something real and true, and perhaps more close
to Bethlehem than elaborately rehearsed pageants and well-
trained choirs. "Except ye become as little children." How
I wish some of my city friends whose Christmas programs
were the last word in finish had been able to share in that
simple, crude, and lovely Christmas "concert" in that little
hot kitchen, with the marsh behind the house leading down
to the wintry sea, and the clear stars shining through the
frosty air.

ELEVEN

THE GUZZLE IS A ROAD THAT FOLLOWS A STREAM BACK INTO the wilderness away from Route 1. The first time I drove it I was sure it had been named in the spring, for the wheels of the car sank deep in the mud as the road wound down to a low bridge across the rushing water, then twisted and climbed the hill only to find again deep ruts of clay and alder bushes close enough to scratch the car. In June one stops there by the bridge to watch the ceaseless darting of the swallows: tree swallows, barn swallows, and eave swallows in great numbers dart back and forth in their wide-mouthed search for the insects that rise above the water there by the dam. Usually a phoebe announces his presence as he sits perched waiting for his supper to fly by. The place is alive with myrtle warblers and redstarts, and dizzying swoops of blue-backed swallows. Such a fluttering of birds. Farther up, at the very end of the guzzle, the stream broadens out into a tranquil pond where wood ducks with

their gorgeous plumage may be seen. "Henrietta" lives "up the guzzle." She had asked me to supper.

I found a large square farmhouse, weather-beaten and entirely without paint. Sheds and barns were attached to the main house in a long rambling structure. Just beyond the barn was a woodshed piled full of firewood and close behind the buildings the forest came in like a high tide of wilderness. On that first visit, which must have been in early spring, I heard the woodcock "beeping" in the dusk, and it seemed as if at any moment deer might come out from the forest shelter to seek a late frozen apple still clinging to the wintry branches of the half-wild trees behind the house.

But inside all was cozy and cheerful. A fine fire in the kitchen range heated the large kitchen. One entered through the woodshed, though there is a front door, reserved for funerals and never used for anything else. Off the kitchen to one side was a bedroom, where I laid my coat, and beyond, through the kitchen, was the "front room." One could guess that this was a masculine sort of household, for over the door to the bedroom was a gun rack of deer hooves with two businesslike rifles on it, and in the front room a mounted deer head on each side flanked the big bay window that looked out on the road. Set in the bay window was a green tub with an enormous Christmas cactus. Henrietta said it had had one hundred and sixty blossoms that winter. I visited there a bit with "Grandma Lillie," whose lameness made walking difficult but whose cheerfulness rose above much pain. I found her a wonderful old lady, full of tart observations about life and great common sense and a fierce loyalty and devotion to her church, along with a spirit that rebelled against the frustrations of arthritis. If her legs had been equal to her spunk there would have been nothing she wouldn't tackle.

Presently the meal was ready and I sat down to the kitchen table with "Henny," a large motherly woman with an enthusiasm equal to her mother's and a warmhearted vitality that made anything good seem possible. Henny's "menfolks" were her husband—a fisherman with a tanned weather-beaten face, clear eye, and silent manner that was both friendly and reserved (he gave the impression that he didn't think much of talk just for the sake of conversation, but when he had something to say he would be ready to say it)—and one of the grown sons, almost as silent as his father. Two other sons were in Korea.

The table was spread with a clean cloth and on it were plates of hot and fluffy biscuits and great plates of lobster stew. Never have I seen such stew, so full of lobster meat one could hardly find the milk! With its steaming red-gold color and delicious smell it was food for the gods. I had to pinch myself to remember about the "forlorn little churches" I was supposed to be serving. Here was food that couldn't be found in the most luxurious clubs or restaurants of our biggest cities at any price. The lobster meat was sweet and fresh, Henny's husband, Harold, had brought it in that noon, the biscuits just out of the oven, the tea sturdy. We heard the whispering of wind outside in the pine trees, the sound of the turbulent stream and the "beeping" of woodcock in the alder growth.

Henny's faith is forthright and simple. Her trust in her pastor is a bit frightening. She comes out with direct questions about matters of deep theological import—such as why the good so often have to suffer while those whose lives are not helpful to the community, nor expressive of faith, seem to have such an easy time. I replied: "Of course no one can possibly know, really, but as far as I can see, it is one of the proofs that this life is not the end of the story. And however unfair things may seem to be we can always remember that the Lord God did not spare his own Son, even though his life was perfectly blameless. We don't know the spiritual laws by which our soul's growth is refined, but we can be sure of the Love behind the mystery and must trust it." What other answer can one make?

And in childlike simplicity she replied, "Oh, I see. So that's how it is. Somebody asked me and I didn't know what to say, so I wanted to ask you."

When the District Superintendent came for his Quarterly Conference with the church Henny asked us both to dinner. It was in the autumn and the meal, of course, was deer meat. Such venison I never tasted, tender, sweet, rich, and so packed full of iron you could fairly feel the red blood corpuscles shout. All this completed by flaky apple pie. It was not only for the quality of her faith and the excellence of her food that I came to love Henny as my own sister. She had a penetrating insight into people and their ways. With one sentence she could go to the heart of a situation and know what to do about it. Her love for her church made her "stand up to" those less hardy souls who thought the struggle to keep the church going just too hard. Henny was a one-man powerhouse, and the church stayed open. When it was time for Conference she would attend, often the only lay delegate from this entire section. She listened with keen interest and came back sighing, "If only the others would go to Conference they would feel different about their church!"

Life on the back-country roads seems to build sturdiness into the women as well as into the men. There is probably nobody in this whole section more beloved and respected than Susy—and "Susy" she is to the people for miles around, and to the fishermen and hunters who rent her camps from April through November. She and her husband, "Big Chief" Stanwood, live on a narrow neck of land between two of the finest lakes for salmon and trout fishing anywhere around. On "Little Tunk" only fly fishing is allowed. Those who use worms or other bait must cross the narrow bit of land and fish in the larger lake whose outlet stretches back some seven miles to the State Camp Ground at the outlet. Susy's language is as forthright as her thinking. She has no place in her heart for sham or pretense and she is kindness itself. As she puts it, "I'd rather do things when I can for people—get more fun out of it—than be growlin' about it." I think I'd rather incur the wrath of all the district superintendents and bishops of the church than lose the respect and regard of Susy Stanwood. There is something about her as crystal-clear as the spring water she dips up for her guests, and she expects that clarity from all with whom she deals. I think the initial interview with Saint Peter must be something like facing Susy.

One day she called me about a young family that had moved into town. There was a new baby expected. The young father, just a boy, had evidently never learned much about responsibility; they were trying to make a home in a two-room shack without lights or any conveniences at all. Susy expressed herself forcibly about neighbors who would criticize a fellow when he was down but wouldn't do anything to help, told me she had "heard only hearsay" but she had heard plenty. She couldn't go investigate without being "nosy" but I could go, as pastor and see what the situation was. "Let me know what's needed. I guess you and I'll see that those kids get a break," she ended. I looked at the telephone wire to see if it had melted under the heat of her indignation!

I went out and found a lot of independence and pride in the young couple, whose two children seemed well and happy. The father was bringing two pails of water from a spring across the road. He had a pathetic sign nailed to the tree by the house, announcing that he was an auto mechanic and would repair anything. I wondered how in the world he could think anyone would seek him out on this lonely road for a repair job. He assured me that he could cut enough firewood from the young birch and "popple" growing behind the cabin, and that he was going to have steady work in a few days cutting wood for the sawmill. The only immediate need that I could spot was a crib for the younger of the two children, who had already outgrown the bassinet that would be needed for the newcomer. The older little girl, about four, could sleep in the bed.

The electric light company was willing to turn the lights on again when I told them I would pay for the deposit on the meter, and the service charge for the connections, though they were obviously wondering whether the young man would meet his bill when it came due. So was I. But I couldn't feel right about having the new baby come back to a new house with no lights. Lamps are just too dangerous where there are young children. Susy provided baby clothes and blankets; soon other neighbors were showing real interest and several fine boxes of groceries were sent in. When

Susy takes hold of a situation we all fall in line. What a general she would make!

One day she called me on the phone. "Mrs. Henrichsen, there's a couple out here want to get married." This was a Saturday morning.

"Well, send them in to see me," I suggested. I could hear a very flat silence at the other end of the telephone.

"You couldn't come out here this afternoon?" Then I realized that Susy wanted to have a part in it.

"Why I guess I could," I said. "What about these people, Susy? Do they know what they are doing?"

"Oh yes." Her voice was strong and hearty. "I've known them both a long time. They're all right."

So the hour was set and I went out across the hills and the cutover "blueberry land"—down the long road that penetrated the very heart of the forest and out to the fishing camp, with the two lakes sparkling in the spring sunshine and the wind in the pines making lovely caressing noises. To my amazement, when I entered the long low building, I found that the couple were Indians. The man was a chief who made his livelihood by giving lectures to schools and community groups about Indian lore. His copper-colored face was wreathed in smiles, his English cultivated and fine. He wore a number of rings of beautiful silver and turquoise work, the sort of thing one expects in Navajo country but hardly in Maine. His bride also had on beautiful, heavy silver jewelry—bracelets and an intricate necklace. He had traveled all over the United States and had a wonderful collection of Kodachrome slides, some of which he showed me after the wedding.

Susy introduced us and we talked for a few minutes about

the meaning of the ceremony. I looked over their papers, which were in order, and I felt that they were both intelligent and sincere in their devotion, mature people who would make their marriage succeed. We were just about ready to start when in came two fishermen for information about flies and fishing spots. They wanted to rent some boats. So we stalled, making small talk until the fishermen left. Then we held the wedding service. After they had been pronounced "husband and wife together" and we had had the final prayer and benediction, Susy invited me to stay for supper with them. Since it was Saturday and it was Maine, supper meant baked beans, brown bread, and cabbage salad! Not even a wedding feast can disturb Down East tradition for Saturday night menus. I wonder how many ministers have been invited to that sort of "wedding supper" —at one end of a long table in a fishing camp, with a full-blooded Indian chief smiling down at his shy bride.

One of my favorite stories of this back country was told me by the lawyer across the street, who has a memory stored with wonderful incidents from his boyhood as well as from the vagaries of human nature as seen in a law office. Some years ago a matter came up for litigation. An old fellow took his "squatter's rights" right into court.

In an unincorporated township this man had built himself a cabin and lived there for seven or eight years. He felt that he owned the country around his cabin, and there was no one to argue the point. Although his cabin was a long way from the nearest village, he walked the miles to voice a grievance. With all that open country to choose from, a man had come in and settled, so he said, right in his very dooryard. He wanted the intruder ousted. The judge listened patiently to his tirade and then said, "Now sir, to get at the facts of this a bit better, just how close to your house would you say this fellow had put his cabin?"

And the indignant squatter replied, "Every bit as near as ten mile it is!"—and that was right in his dooryard!

Yes, there's room for a man to be independent in a land like this if "that's his mind."

How much of this wilderness country there is hereabout I became aware of one spring. My brother wrote me to see if I could find any old oxbows. He had an idea that oxbows could be made into effective lighting fixtures for his Montana ranch and hoped I could find some for him in old farms and barns.

From one farm to another they sent me on this search. Somebody would say, "Have you asked so-and-so? His father used to drive a team of oxen, one of the last teams around here. I should think he'd likely have some of the bows." So I would go to see so-and-so and usually found that he didn't have any but thought that up over the hill at somebody else's place I'd "most prob'ly" find what I was looking for.

The first of the bows I found was very old, very heavy. The beaten iron ring that hung from the center was rusted deep and there was a wide crack through the bow. How the patient beasts had ever carried such a weight on their shoulders, much less dragged a sled by it, I could not imagine. Up at another farm I found two very small ones that had been used for training young steers. I finally ended up with seven in various stages of preservation—hardly any two the same size. I had given anywhere from one dollar to five for them, though two were given me for nothing at all —"They h'aint no good to us, just in the way. Take 'em if you want 'em and welcome." It cost more to crate and ship them than they were worth. My brother says they add enormous prestige to the ranch, for there in the golden West, Eastern oxbows are rare indeed and men have been known to pay forty dollars for a single bow! What would my neighbors think of that? They thought I was slightly touched to offer four dollars for useless junk that was just "clutterin' up the barn loft."

One of the places where I had first gone in search of the bows was out to the end of the Molasses Pond road, where it climbs up Sugar Hill. This sweet-tooth-named country is a maple-sugar-producing section, and the finest syrup I have ever eaten comes from the farm at the end of the road. Each March I go out to get several quarts of the clear golden-brown syrup and send it to the Montana brother, as well as to friends. All of California's glamor cannot produce this delectable essence of granite hill, winter snow, and spring sunshine.

There is much besides poetry, heroism, and gentlehearted kindness in these back-country homes. Sometimes there is feeble-mindedness, sometimes poverty that is unnecessary and cruel, often tragedy of one sort or another. On one hidden road there lived a family in a fairly large shingle-and-tarpaper house. There were several children. One day I went out to call, making my way through the mud, over the various toys, around a barking puppy tied to a tree, and so into the kitchen. I am sure the temperature in that kitchen must have been well over ninety; it was like opening a blast furnace when I stepped inside. Three of the children seemed quite normal, though the baby was so very white that I feared for it. Two of the children had not taken off their snowsuits and the baby was very warmly dressed—no wonder it was white in that terrible heat. The fourth baby, a little girl about two and a half, was not talking, only making incoherent sounds. She was obviously abnormal, her large head and face badly discolored with a deep-red birthmark. Poor child, I thought, what chance does she have? But as I visited I noticed the tender solicitude of the mother for this handicapped little one, as if by the very strength of her love she would shield it from the fierce struggle of life.

Perhaps a year later I was called to the home. This child had died. The grief of the father and mother was real and deep. The father sat bowed behind the stove, suffering silently—a figure of sorrow before the double mystery of life and death, and the strange accident that might have made life so very hard for his little girl if she had lived to grow up. The mother smiled through her tears as she said she knew it was the love of the Heavenly Father that had taken her baby out of a world that would have been just too hard for her.

But the depth of heartbreak for me was in her starry-eyed wonder as she came to church for the service. The little girl, in a lovely pink dress with pleated skirt and patent leather shoes and white socks, lay in the tiny casket like a beautiful doll. Her face was white and clear, the only time the mother had ever seen it that way, and as she looked at the little body she turned to me whispering in awe, "My baby is beautiful, my baby is beautiful!"

TWELVE

THE COMMUNITY WAS HUSHED. PEOPLE SPOKE SOFTLY AND with a gentle undertone. Word had come to us that Mrs. Schieffelin had died in her New York home. "There'll never be another like her," they said, and for days when people met at the post office or the store there was a loving spirit of remembering together things she had said and done. Even the most silent and noncommittal of our men ventured the remark, "She'll be missed." From him it was an eloquent tribute. We learned of the hour when her farewell service would be held at the Madison Avenue Presbyterian Church in New York and planned a memorial service for that same afternoon at the same hour. The little chapel was filled, the spirit of loving remembering and triumphant faith was there. We felt as if she must know, and as if she were there with us, as she was in our hearts. We sang hymns that had been her special favorites, and on the anniversary Sunday each year we still sing those same hymns: "Dear Lord and Father

of Mankind," "Immortal Love, Forever Full," "For All the Saints." They speak to us of her own strong and vital faith as well as of the God whom she loved, served, and trusted.

The next year the wife of her oldest son told me that the family and friends would like to establish some sort of memorial for Mrs. Schieffelin in our village, and asked if I thought people would like to have some redecoration of the little chapel. This was a project in which we could all have a part, summer friends, family, and year-round folk. The more we thought about it, the more enthusiastic we became. Presently, under her wise leadership, plans were being formed.

From the very start this was entered into by the whole Ashville Community. Local men did the work and before winter came we were stripping the embossed metal off the walls, preparatory to covering them with sheetrock. Where there had been an elaborate curve connecting wall and ceiling we put a simple dentiled molding. We painted the interior a white that was just "off white," not the shining white of a hospital, not "oyster" gray, but a white that was clear and clean yet somehow warm and soft. It didn't happen in a minute. All winter we watched the work go forward and sometimes wondered if the mess ever would be cleaned up again. But at least we were rid of the flyspecked Ten Commandments!

Of one thing we were sure, now we must have pews instead of folding chairs. But if we put pews in the church and made the sanctuary really worshipful, where would we hold quilting bees, church suppers, Sunday School? Transformation of the basement into a vestry seemed to be the answer. The women of the church took this on as their project, and a major operation it was, for the basement was

almost entirely filled with a huge wood-burning furnace set
on a solid concrete foundation. When spring came, and we
could do without the heat, that furnace was taken out and
the concrete block chipped away. Asphale tile flooring, light
walls, and clean windows made the room much lighter.
The old iron stove and cupboards were torn out and at the
farther end of the room a new and modern set of cupboards
and shelves were put in. In this unit was also a "dry sink"
with a fitted board that covered it when not in use. Some of
the cupboards were devoted to dishes and silver for church
suppers, others given over to Sunday School supplies. On
Sundays pictures, candles, a cross were set up as a worship
center on this shelf. At the back an oil burner was put in, and
a floor furnace installed to heat the upstairs. We had a small
stove fed by bottled gas that was adequate for making
coffee, warming cooked dishes, or heating dishwater. It was
a very usable room. For several winters we held our church
services there in the worst weather, as well as Sunday School,
in order to conserve heat and keep snow, slush, and mud off
the newly refinished floor upstairs. Now that we have a good
community meeting place we have organized a farm bureau
which with other groups uses our "recreation room." It has
even been used by private groups for such things as wedding
and baby showers. Once a month there is a church supper
and get-together, and the feeling of understanding and
mutual appreciation has grown perceptibly. How pleased
Mrs. Schieffelin would be!

Finding the pews for the Sanctuary posed a problem.
Over in the little community of West Franklin was a church
literally tumbling down. Its windows were out, its roofs
leaked. There was no possibility of its being restored. The
community was tiny and those who had any interest in

church could easily go to either of the two churches in Franklin. My first summer I had held a few services there, almost outdoor services, and it was lovely to see that white pigeons had nested in the belfry and, as in mediaeval paintings, were always hovering there as if to indicate the blessing of God. But just the same, it was pathetic to see decay of this place of worship, and the people were generally agreed that it would be better to take the church down than to let it fall down, or perhaps become a bonfire. So we applied for permission to buy the pews. Well built they were, and of good material.

Negotiations took some time. Families of the original pew owners had to be reached. In these country churches it had been the custom for people to own their pews. Money for church construction had been raised in this manner and some of them even held deeds to this property. Many of the original owners had died. Some of their descendants could not be located. But eventually the necessary permissions were obtained and we found ourselves with fifteen good pews for which we had paid the enormous sum of five dollars apiece! The next winter one of the local men sanded and repainted them—using the same white as the walls, keeping the dark mahogany line at the back and down the arms of each one.

We wanted to change the piano and put in its place a small organ. All through the countryside were reed organs, the so-called "parlor organs" of our grandmother's day, so we spoke to one man who carried on a lively trade in the old Yankee tradition. One of the fine musicians of our summer colony, the New York organist Dr. Isadore Freed, had told me that this man was a good judge of organs and

skilled in their repair and upkeep. Our trader said he thought
he could find the organ we wanted. In fact he thought he
had it in his barn at that moment.

With characteristic friendliness, he said that since it was
for the church he would charge us just ten dollars, the cost
to him of replacing some reeds and putting it in order. When
it didn't arrive at the promised time, we began to wonder
and finally found that he had had trouble getting a truck
and someone to help him load and unload it. This accom-
plished, he said that without fail we would have it the next
Sunday, but when I arrived at church it was not in place.
What more could we say? At that low price we were not in a
position to be too insistent. When I got to Gouldsboro church
that same afternoon, there was the organ, safely delivered
to the wrong church—which already had two such organs!

Again, he had to get his friend with the truck, but the
Ashville Community felt that since it was his mistake, they
should not pay for the second truck trip. It is not often that
our trading friend loses on a deal, but I am certain that he
must have been out of pocket on this one. However, with
his wonderful good humor, he probably accepts it philo-
sophically and chalks it up as a contribution, nonetheless
generous because inadvertent, to the church work.

The light fixture certainly had to be changed. We had
a large hanging globe in the center of the church, filled
with dead moths and flies, which was a great dirt collector
and eyesore. The Schieffelin family made a wonderful suggestion. Mr. Schieffelin had moved into a smaller apartment.
There were wall sconces available that we might have if
we wished. What a help that was! Two were in the form of
eagles, the others were plain; each held two candle-like light

bulbs. Simple, gold-finished, they were placed between the windows, the eagle fixtures at the front of the church behind the pulpit and lectern, which had also been painted white with mahogany trim. It seems appropriate that light fixtures which Mrs. Schieffelin had used so often should be in this little church, for her friendship had brought light to so many lives here.

Finally the essentials were done, although there was still much to be finished. We needed a bit more money, and one of the other summer residents made a fine offer. Her friend, the famous pianist Clara Rabinovitch, was coming. Would we like to have a benefit concert? She would prevail on her friend to play and we could hold the concert in her boathouse. I had never been in the boathouse, but knowing Mrs. Spring and the unusual and lovely things that were in her own house, I felt sure that the boathouse would be an interesting place for such a recital. So we printed and distributed invitations, to the people of our own community and to many summer friends in nearby places. People came from Hancock, Blue Hill, even Bar Harbor and Northeast Harbor, and so there were about one hundred and thirty of them gathered there in the "boathouse" that held no boats, but a wonderful collection of Shaker furniture. It was on a wooded point close to the edge of the water, and those who preferred to sat out on the lawn where they could enjoy the view and the soft scent of pines and spruce while listening to wonderful music—Ravel, Debussy, Mozart, Chopin, Schumann, Bach—played with eager spontaneous verve as well as perfect musicianship.

No tickets were sold; an offering was taken and found to be nearly two hundred dollars. Mrs. Spring was as delighted as a child that her project had been so successful, and when we implied that her sponsorship, the lovely place, and the delicious punch and sandwiches that she served had something to do with it, as well as the generosity of the artist, she would not agree but in real self-effacement felt it was all due to the love of the countryside for Mrs. Schieffelin.

A year later it was decided that the narrow concrete steps leading into the church should be replaced by broad steps of our native granite. Mr. and Mrs. Schieffelin, Jr., went to the quarry and picked out two beautiful slabs, which give a fine air of welcome. And then Mrs. Spring made us a present of hand-wrought iron railings to complete the entrance.

Mrs. Spring's simplicity and unexpected enthusiasms are legendary and in her own right she is deeply loved. Naturally very shy, she has not entered so fully into the life of the whole community as the Schieffelin family, but her own household staff is devoted to her, and her perception of what things will make life easier for others and her delight in providing those things are indeed rare. One of the former residents of the town said of Mr. Spring during his lifetime—and it could equally well be said of her—"He's common, just as common as I am. Acts as if he ain't no better than I am—and of course he ain't—not a mite!"

Mrs. Spring makes us all feel our common humanity, but unfortunately her spirit is far from "common": it would be a happier world if that generosity were not so rare. She often makes a present of some very useful and thoughtful object, saying, "If you don't want this, give it to somebody you don't like!" It's a safe suggestion. Whether the gift is a very necessary article of furniture or a ten-cent notebook, it carries with it such warmth and such desire to be helpful that you wouldn't dream of parting with it and simply hope to learn from her the art of genuine giving.

Eventually the chapel was finished and reflected the unerring taste as well as the months of work of Mrs. Schieffelin's daughter-in-law, who had worked so unobtrusively that everyone felt it was his own project; all were unitedly happy about the results. The altar was covered with a lovely deep-maroon velvet and behind it hung a reredos curtain of the same material with the simple cross placed upon it. At the windows were hangings of clear daffodil-yellow. With the white walls and white pews, there was a feeling of triumphant peace here suggesting an Easter lily, truly a fitting memorial for Mrs. Schieffelin. Mr. Schieffelin offered two carved straight-backed hall chairs of fumed oak; the white wall shows through the carving and the design takes away the austerity the room might otherwise have had. He also presented to the chapel a low brass bowl, shaped like an old Roman lamp, and a pair of three-branched brass candlesticks, which are placed on either side of it. Now the chapel was complete and plans were made for the rededication service.

It was to be held on the anniversary of Mrs. Schieffelin's death, a Friday. To our joy we found that the Bishop could come. Dr. Henry P. Van Dusen, long-time friend of the family and a summer member of the community, was here. We asked him to speak on the place of the church in community life. Dr. Henry Sloane Coffin, before his retirement Dr. Van Dusen's predecessor as President of Union Theological Seminary, was to be present, for he had been Mrs. Schieffelin's pastor and lifelong friend in New York City. We asked him to give the memorial address. The Bishop would perform the act of rededication. But one couldn't ask the Bishop without asking the District Superintendent. After all, this was in his District, so we asked him to read the Scripture. As the local pastor it was my task to open the service with the call to worship and the invocation. Poor little church, I wondered how it could bear up under such an influx of clergy. I doubt if a one-room church, seating perhaps eighty people at the very outside, ever had so many prominent theologians to help in its dedication. I felt as if we ought to make more of the occasion, perhaps parade through the village streets as was customary in the Middle Ages! And after the service was over, I noticed still another cleric who should have been recognized, the President of the Virginia Theological Seminary, Dr. Zabriskie, was seated in the congregation. People from miles around, as well as the entire local neighborhood, came with an overwhelming feeling of thanksgiving and love.

The service, with appropriate Scriptures, Mrs. Schieffelin's favorite hymns, those truly inspiring addresses by Dr. Van Dusen and Dr. Coffin, and the beautiful and simple solemnity of the act of dedication as performed by Bishop John Wesley Lord of the Methodist Church, led up to a fine climax as one of Mrs. Schieffelin's little brown-eyed great-granddaughter's unveiled the tablet while her oldest son read the words of the inscription:

To the Glory of God,
and in loving memory of
Maria Louisa Shepard Schieffelin
whose living faith inspired her family
and friends to renovate this chapel
that it may increase in service
to God and man

And somehow from that moment the little chapel did take **on a** new feeling. A year or two later the visiting nurse said **to me,** "What's happened to Ashville? The whole community has perked up."

And I could honestly reply, "Yes, now they have a church of which they are proud." I think Mrs. Schieffelin would have nodded her head under its crown of white hair, her brown eyes shining. Perhaps she knows.

It was the same man whose comment about Mr. Spring was so typical of our Down East independence of spirit who once justified a delayed letter.

But to tell the story I should first describe "The Ravens." They are two delightful ladies from Baltimore, Mrs. Thomsen and Miss Sawyer, her sister. Their house, which once belonged to their great-grandfather, sits far back from the road at the Tunk Lake corner. It is of simple white clapboards and of fine proportions. The circular drive sweeps up to the front door past perfectly kept flower beds of nasturtiums and petunias, sweet peas, roses, bachelor buttons, and gladiolas, their particular specialty. The flower beds are kept as spotless as the house, and at daybreak "Miss Mary" is out with wide hat and gloves to do battle with the slugs.

Inside there is an atmosphere of coolness and serenity, no matter how hot the day. The old braided rugs, wide paneling, mahogany furniture, old prints, and, in the hall, the wallpaper with an open pattern of pine branches, all express perfectly the restraint and love of the beautiful which shows itself in fine thinking and generous action as well as in surroundings. All through the war years and the years of hardship which followed for Europe, these two ladies assembled and packed countless boxes for Holland, England, and other countries, every box so carefully put together, so many intricate knots so strongly tied. Many younger and more vigorous people would have felt they had done well at having done far less. Perfectionists for themselves, "The Ravens" are tolerant and amused by others whose standards are not their own.

I have called them the Ravens ever since I discovered their passion for feeding any prophets (or would-be prophets) they can get hold of. Someone once said, "They collect ministers the way others collect antiques." For some years now it has been the tradition on Sunday nights in the summer for me to stop at their house on my way home for a "let-down"—rest, a chance to talk over the day, and food; sandwiches, ginger ale, ice cream or a wonderful jello concoction full of cherries and covered with whipped cream, or perhaps strawberries.

But best of all, conversation. Understanding, delightful conversation. Sometimes wise counsel about local situations —for the ladies have known my year-round people for a lifetime and are most tactful in making suggestions. They are discreet and fine. One can talk intimately with them about problems and know that confidences are not violated. And they have a quick humor which helps restore balance by seeing the funny side of things.

It was they who wrote the letter to a friend in a nearby Maine town, a letter which was twelve days in reaching its destination. Since it should have been at the most an overnight trip, even allowing for delays—not more than a two-day trip they went to the postmaster to protest and ask gently how it happened.

And the reply was this. "When did you mail it?"

"It was noon," said Miss Mary, naming the day. "I remember because you had gone home to dinner and we put it through the slot into the box," she indicated the low open box on the inside of the post office door.

"Oh, that explains it," he said. "That was the day the cat had her kittens in the box, and we didn't like to disturb her until they were old enough to be taken out."

THIRTEEN

VACATION TIME WAS COMING, NOT IN THE SUMMER BUT IN FEB-
ruary. After much consultation it was decided that was the
best time for me to be away. In the summer the work was
much too busy—our population more than doubles in two of
the towns. Besides, who would want to leave the Maine coast
in the summer for anywhere else? But by February the
church woodpiles were getting low, people were tired of
shoveling out. There was no really good time to go, but I
knew that I needed a recharging of the spiritual batteries.
Dr. Van Dusen had suggested that I come to Union Theological Seminary for at least a part of the vacation and I was
looking forward eagerly to the contact with keen minds, the
very best theological thinking that could be found, and a
chance for the perspective that distance gives.

I was to have three Sundays away, and that gave me nearly
four weeks. I made a plane reservation for Monday morning.
On Sunday, speaking to the little group at Gouldsboro

church, I told of my plan. Myrtle Archer, one of the stalwart
souls of the church, said, "That's a long time to be away." If
she had said it a year or two earlier I would have thought it
a protest—that she thought I ought not to take so much time.
But now that I knew these Down East folk better, I knew
that what she was saying was, "It will seem long to us."
Affection is real though deeply camouflaged.

So I replied, "Oh you'll appreciate me all the more when
I get back."

Quick as a flash she retorted, "I dunno's we shall. It all
depends on how you behave!" And that too was affection!

But that evening as I started for Prospect Harbor it was
snowing hard, a fine dry snow driven by strong winds. It had
a businesslike feel. This was no "flurry." All the way down
through those dark woods I thought to myself, This is a real
storm—you're silly to try to come. I half hoped there would
be no one at the church, so that I could turn around and
come back before it got any worse. But as I rounded the
corner and parked the car I saw the lighted windows and
heard the singing with which they used the time before I
arrived. And when I stepped inside I saw twenty-three
people. These were no "fair-weather Christians."

As the service progressed I could hear the wind and the
beat of the stinging snow against the windows, and I felt
very sure that unless the morning was very clear no planes
would be flying out of Bangor. Oh well! It didn't matter too
much. I could go later and it would be nice to have a day at
home to catch up on many things before I left.

When we came out of church we could hardly see the road
or the parked cars. The wind was not only driving the snow
in a blinding gale but it was also piling up drifts. I got to the
car, wondering if it would start. It did, but in the white swirl-

ing world there was little visibility and as I turned around in front of the school, where I thought there was plenty of room, the car slid and slipped and settled in the deep, snow-filled ditch. One of the men had waited to see if I got out all right and when he saw the situation we agreed that nothing could be done about it that night in the blizzard. "You'll have to come home with us for the night," he said, opening the truck door. And I was glad to.

I thought of the parsonage getting colder and colder as the wood fire, built up before I left, died out for lack of fuel, and of my black Toby dog, successor to the first two, whose lives had come to a full fourteen years and who had in those years given a "last full measure of devotion" such as only a good dog can. Toby must be cold and bewildered. But there was nothing I could do but stay and not worry.

My host and hostess were wonderful. They made me comfortable in their friendly guest room and assured me that I was lucky that the trouble came in the village rather than halfway home through the woods. I knew they were right.

Unfortunately for me, I had worn that day a dress that was both too tight and too short. I had wanted to save my better clothes for the New York trip and I had figured that under my robe it wouldn't matter too much. But to my dismay the next morning it was still snowing just as hard. The roads were drifted in great drifts, nothing was moving, the snowplows hadn't even tried to get out and I was definitely a prisoner of the snow. It was good to be in such a friendly home but I could hardly feel relaxed, for as we all sat in the living room I was very much aware of the skintight, too short dress and tried to make myself as small as possible—a completely futile attempt.

By afternoon the snowing had stopped and the sun was

out, a sparkling brilliance making clean blue shadows between acres of diamonds. But the wind was continuing, making the ever mounting drifts something to see. The snowplow came through once and the snow blew back behind it almost immediately. I tried telephoning to Sullivan, that the operator might know I was safe, for I suspected that the neighbors would notice the open garage door and know I had not got home. She connected me with one neighbor, Dwight. I asked him if he thought he could get out of his yard that afternoon and told him of my predicament. He agreed that he thought he could get out and said he would go to the house, let the dog out for a bit, and build up a new fire so that the pipes wouldn't freeze by a second night without heat. He also agreed to feed Toby and see that he had fresh water.

Tuesday morning my host and some of the other men went down to the church and putting heavy chains on a big truck, they managed to pull my car out of the ditch, none the worse for its nights in the open. I got home from Sunday night service by Tuesday noon! Dwight had most thoughtfully dug out a car length of my drifted driveway so that I could get the car off the road, and by Friday the sun and warming weather had brought the drifts down to manageable proportions so we could shovel out. It was a week later when I finally got off for my vacation.

What a different life from our woods and villages and our simplicities it was to step into the heart of New York City. And what welcome and warmth of friendship I found there. Union Theological Seminary is across the street from Riverside Church, and from the guest room window I could get a glimpse of the Hudson River. My room was almost under the great tower of Riverside Church with its wonderful carillon. I seemed surrounded by beautiful Gothic architecture. The Seminary buildings form a quadrangle, along one side of which is an arched cloister. In the lovely chapel are stained-glass windows. In the house the paneling is of oak. Even the doors in the Seminary building have bronze crosses on the plates which hold the doorknobs, reminders of One who said, "I am the door." It was all a perfect setting for churchly study and for personal devotion and meditation, for everywhere one saw symbols of faith.

The guest room was about as big as the whole downstairs of my parsonage. It contained beautiful mahogany furniture, twin beds, highboy, bureau, chaise longue, desk, fireplace. I felt as if it were quarters that should be reserved for archbishops at least. Beyond the lovely room with its cheerful deep-red curtains that were pulled across the leaded windows at night, was my own bathroom, white-tiled and spotless. Across the hall was the handsome formal "drawing room," with Chinese rugs, yellow damask-covered sofa, old blue Canton ware in the recessed cupboards on either side of the fireplace, books and curios in a Sheraton bookcase, and a piano.

On the street floor under my room was the dining room, and across the hall, under the drawing room, was the family living room, formal and dignified yet at the same time cozy and livable. It takes rare skill to convey both feelings at once and Mrs. Van Dusen has that sort of skill. In the halls were beautiful oil paintings of Scottish scenes which she had done and everywhere were interesting touches suggestive of out-of-the-way places: an African mask in the dining room, precious bits of Chinese white jade on the mantel, a Celtic rune over the living room fireplace, carved wooden figures from Nigeria, and everywhere books.

But beyond the churchly and beautiful surroundings was the opportunity for contact with great minds and great souls. Dr. Van Dusen took the trouble to see that I had a copy of the Seminary catalog and a schedule of classes and told me which ones he thought I might find especially interesting. I had the "keys to the city" and an open invitation to go into any class and "sit in" at any lecture. It was exciting. Not only were the professors gracious to this stranger but the students were cordial and friendly, the Seminary staff went out of their several ways to be helpful, and Mr. James Anderson, the smiling and able handler of details in the "general office," was most obliging, arranging for me to rent a typewriter, supplying me with necessary information, and all the while calling me "Doctor" in spite of my repeated protests that I was not a doctor—just plain Mrs. Henrichsen.

I found that certain classes were more immediately useful for my need than others. Some of them did not give, in isolated lectures, enough that one could use without the continuity of what came before and what was to come after, though these, too, had their value in mind-stretching and the opening of new avenues of thought. Others were intensely stimulating. I found myself longing to be twenty-five instead of fifty, so that I might begin from the beginning and study the Bible in the original Hebrew and Greek. The professors in those subjects gave fascinating glimpses of the added richness and meaning that could be understood only in the original tongues. They told me of a new Biblical commentary in progress, *The Interpreter's Bible,* which would contain many fresh insights and detailed expositions of each passage. I decided then and there that I could somehow manage to save the hundred dollars it would cost to have that book. Not only would it give the meanings of the text but it would give the thinking of the best preachers of our day about these Scriptures.

The classes in preaching, each Tuesday, were a lively experience. At least three different professors took those hours and I have at various times visited them all. Such good sermon outlines as these students presented! It was an inspiration to listen to this teaching by Dr. Bowie, Dr. Scherer, Dr. McCracken, and Dr. Buttrick. But valuable as the instruction was, the most helpful point about these classes was to see the patience and wisdom with which these great teachers handled their students. Outlines of sermons were put on the board and commented on by the class. Then these men helped the young preachers to take their sermons apart, find their good points, take out or change the weak ones, put it together again in stronger form and somehow come up with an effective and clear presentation. Dr. Buttrick had a trick of clapping a student on the shoulder with a word of commendation that was like an accolade. No matter how many criticisms had been made of the sermon in its original form, when the hour was over the boy had a creditable piece of work to use. Moreover, though his work may have been pretty well picked apart, his self-respect had been built up and his confidence strengthened. It was an experience of being in the presence of the Holy Spirit as He works through a greathearted teacher to reach the mind of each conscientious, eager disciple.

One of the most wonderful parts of life at the Seminary was the daily chapel service. How good it was to be a worshiper in the pews at these daily services, sometimes led by students, sometimes by faculty members, sometimes by outside speakers. And that choir, expertly trained, singing great hymns with beauty of tone and interpretation as well as with sincerity of feeling. When I was asked if I would take one of those chapel services, it was with a deep feeling of gratitude and humility that I prepared for it—gratitude that even here I was recognized as one of the many many pastors in all parts of the world whom God has called and whom He uses in spite of their weaknesses and sins, and that in this place of worship I could participate as one in that great fellowship. But deeper than the gratitude was the humility as I realized that in this richness of thinking and prayer which pervaded the Seminary atmosphere I had no right to speak unless it was the Holy Spirit who commanded both voice and thought. And I knew perhaps just a little of how very far from Christ's Way my own thinking was. We probably never realize the greatness of that distance—if we did it would paralyze us and we would never speak. But the overwhelming responsibility was almost too much. It was one thing in my own churches, where if I didn't speak the Word given to me there was no one to do it. Here I was faced by the demand for utter sincerity in the face of those who had so much more to give both of wide and deep thought and of consecration. The demand was for a heart free from pride at being in this company, and I was proud to be asked, there was no getting away from it. This brought humiliation of spirit that sent me to my knees, not only in my own room as I worked out the plan for the brief talk but also in the chapel as I entered it quietly for prayer alone the afternoon before.

This vacation plan became the pattern for several years and each year it meant more to me. The week in New York proved to be full of mental stimulation and full of interest in music, museums, and opportunities to see and hear many friends from other days who now live in or near the city. Each year there was a theatre or a movie and one or two

invitations to dinner with old or new friends. An hour out
of New York was the city of my birthplace. On several of
these yearly holidays I spent a weekend there and preached
in the church where I grew up and where my grandfather
had once been pastor. It was good to feel that some of the
old roots still held. One year I spoke to the women of a large
Methodist church in Orange, New Jersey. And each year
I was asked to meet with the students who were especially
interested in serving rural churches, where around a table
we could talk about those details of the minister's work and
relationships which do not lie precisely in the fields of
theological training but are necessary in establishing lasting
helpful human relationships.

One day while I was in New York the telephone rang and
I was told it was a long distance call from Maine. I braced
myself for a summons home, thinking of course that death
or tragedy had visited one of our families. Instead I heard
the voice of a man in a town near my home, but not one
where I have a church. His wife had suddenly left him and
their children. There had been some trouble. He had reason
to suppose she had gone to New York. Could I see if I could
find her?

With dismay I thought of the little town where everybody
knew everybody else, and knew pretty much where they
might be at any given moment, and this teeming city with
its millions. How could I possibly make him understand the
hopelessness of the problem? He told me a little more of the
situation and gave me two names of people they knew in
New York, people with whom she might conceivably have
made some contact if she were there. Assuring him that I
would make an effort, but that I couldn't guarantee finding

her in the first place, or persuading her to return if I did find her, I hung up. He had said that his chief concern was to know that she was all right, and that all he cared about was her happiness. I was glad I could have that to say to her if I should find her, and set about the task.

It took a bit of doing to even locate the names he had given me to call. There are many duplications of common names in the New York telephone book and he had been somewhat vague, in his distraction, about saying where in the city these people might be. The first lead ended in a complete blank. But the second lead was hopeful. Yes—this man had been in touch with her. Yes—he would be seeing her again and he would give her a message. I left my name and telephone number, with the request that she get in touch with me, and waited and hoped and prayed.

And sure enough, the next evening she called and agreed to see me. The Van Dusens, interested in the human need, and generous-hearted as always, had suggested that I invite her for supper and said they would be absent and we could have the meal and a leisurely talk by ourselves.

The delicious dinner helped her past the strangeness of the situation, the peaceful, unstrained atmosphere of the beautiful living room, with a cheerful fire on the hearth, all helped her to feel warm and cared-about instead of frightened and lonely, and it was not too long before she was talking as if she had always known me, about her life at home, the "fed-up-ness" that had been too much for her, and all the matters that had led up to the sudden departure. It didn't take any psychological skill to uncover her real devotion to her children and husband, nor to help her see that those things were even more real than the weariness of spirit that had sent her away. She was more than half ready to return before she ever came to see me, but had worried about how her husband would react and whether he would forgive her. When she knew surely that his whole concern was for her safety and happiness, she wept a bit in relief and contrition, and my own eyes were moist. Our talk had gone deep enough so that we could pray together simply and naturally about it and I could fairly feel the weight roll off her shoulders as she lifted her head again with eyes shining through the tears.

I found that she had never been in a Pullman in her life, and I was glad that I had brought extra emergency money along which would cover her return fare. She was eager for that new adventure of travel. We made the reservation, then we called Maine by long distance, and I went into my room and shut the door so as not to overhear any of the conversation that belonged only to those two. It was just one of God's own miracles that I had been able to locate her at all in the frightening concentration of bewildered and lonely spirits that make up so much of New York.

But all too soon the vacation was over and I was headed back to the airport for my own return. The eyes of the porter nearly popped out of his head as he spotted my enormous fur-trimmed boots on this warm springlike day. But in Maine we had another two months of snow to get through. Although snow doesn't last long in April, we can have storms.

As the plane swept northward I looked down on patches of woods, frozen lakes, and snow-covered hills with eagerness, and when I was met at the airport by the pleasant young man from the garage, with his soft Maine speech and unhurried ways, I was glad all over again that this was the part of the world which was "home." New York had been wonderful. I was rested and stimulated, but awfully glad to get back into work again.

And when a day or two later I was back behind the

wheel of the faithful car on my way to church in the tiny building with its ugly black stove at the back, its need of paint and its forest and seaside setting, and when I looked into the faces of these dear genuine, earnest neighbors of mine, I gave thanks all over again. I doubt if one can appreciate fully churches like these unless one has also had the rich experience of worship in great churches with their glorious choirs, their stained-glass windows, their deep-toned organs and their hundreds of devout worshipers. Either concept of the church is incomplete without the other. And the same God of love and mercy hears the prayers of his children, no matter in what setting they are offered.

Would I ever catch up? The accumulated mail, the accumulated calls, the need to know how things were in each family, were all pushing me but underneath there was the desire to share with my own people the experiences of thought I had had and the deepened insights into the meaning of our faith.

Soon I was back in full harness and the New York days were part of a wonderful store of memories. When the people said to me—and several of them did—"Don't you miss New York and all the wonderful opportunities there?" I could say with perfect honesty, "New York was wonderful, but there is no choice in my mind at all. Here is where I belong." And all the helpful lectures and discussions there gave me no deeper help than the simple act of one of our girls.

It happened the day one of the older women died, a woman whose life had been hard but whose native intelligence was of the keenest. Her shrewd wit and clear thinking were delightful. Her own daughter, restless in temperament and restive under the limitations of an unsatisfactory mar-

riage, had gone away and only recently returned. The house
was in desperate condition. There had been no money for
paint or new sills or other needed repairs. The old lady had
caught a severe cold, pneumonia had set in and malnutri-
tion and advanced age gave it an opportunity that penicillin
could not circumvent. As soon as I heard, I went there. The
undertaker was expected at any moment. The daughter had
found the dress that her mother had saved so carefully all
these years "to be laid away in," but she had found no
clean slip to put on under the dress. In the general confusion of the house it was easy to see how this could be.
Then this other girl came in, a girl whose own life had been
extremely limited, for whom life had been hard in many
ways, and who was really very poor. She heard the discussion and quick as a flash said, "Why, I've got a good slip.
It was given to me for Christmas. I have it on, but it's clean,"
and at once she pulled her dress off over her head, took off
the new taffeta slip, quite probably the only good one she
had ever owned, and slipped her dress back on as the undertaker drove into the yard.

And I, who had several in my bureau drawer at home, had
not even thought of such a thing.

What a blessed education of the heart it is to live among
folk like these!

FOURTEEN

THE CITIZENS OF OUR COMMUNITY WERE ABOUT TO EXERCISE their privileges as members of a democracy. Town Meeting was upon us, and the "warrant" was posted. The Town Report had been printed and distributed to every house-holder. Town Meeting is a big day. The ladies of the church were preparing to serve "Town Meeting dinner" and won-derful supplies of food were solicited and brought in by car after car that drove up to the church vestry. The long tables were set, and all available benches and chairs drawn up. Back in the little kitchen the ladies hovered over the wood-burning range, making the coffee in the big three-gallon coffeepots.

In the Masonic Hall, a mile down the street, the three voting booths had been set up and three of the ladies of the town sat behind the table, registering the voters as they came in. With a flourish the election officer, a tall cheerful man whose conversation took skill to interpret since he had

a cleft palate and stammered besides, drew away the curtain and let the voters into the tiny cubicle. Ballots were marked, then taken to the end of the room where the ballot box was presided over by the town clerk. At twelve o'clock the balloting was closed and everybody adjourned to the vestry for the dinner. As soon as the tables were filled I asked the blessing, and then great bowls of steaming hot beans and plates of brown bread were brought in to tables already garnished with every imaginable sort of pickle and a great array of wonderful salads. When the plates were cleaned the waitress brought in the pies, and there was much fun over asking for a particular kind—"Did Min make that? Then I'll have to have a piece of that one too"—for it was custom to have two or three different kinds, as well as to sample several of the salads. There were plenty of pies to choose from: apple, custard, lemon, mince, squash, chocolate, blueberry, pineapple, banana cream, graham cracker, even cherry and rhubarb made from treasured home-canned supplies. At one o'clock, dinner over, the vestry cleared quickly as people went back to the hall for the chief business of the day.

With a firm bang of the gavel, the Moderator declared the meeting opened and said, "We'll ask Mrs. Henrichsen to say a few words before we begin." This is the standard form for suggesting a prayer. So, walking to the front of the hall, I offered a simple prayer that we might appreciate the freedom we have in this land and recognize that we hold this freedom under God and are responsible to Him for our use of it. Asking that His Spirit direct our decisions and words and all our thinking, and that our town become one where His teachings and His Life are shown in our dealings with each other, I returned to my seat. The first three years here

I had asked the selectmen, quietly, before the meetings, if they would like to have such a prayer and they had "allowed" that they guessed "prob'ly" it "wouldn't hurt none." Now it has become standard procedure, and for some of our people it is the only time when they hear prayer offered—unless it be at a funeral. Alas, many come to Town Meeting who never come to church.

With another bang of the gavel the Moderator read in a clear voice "Article III" (Article I having been concerned with choosing a Moderator and thus taken care of in the morning when the polls opened, and Article II, the election of officers which had already been done by Australian ballot). Many of the Articles are old friends. They recur from year to year and it is almost a singsong as the formula is read: "To see if the town will vote to authorize—", "To see if the town will vote to raise and appropriate—", and especially "To see what sum, if any, the town will vote to raise and appropriate for—"

Snow removal always comes in for some discussion, because of course no one can guess from year to year whether it will be a year of much or little snow. This year, instead of voting to buy a snowplow, the town voted to "let the work of snow removal out on bids." For a good many years a flat sum was voted, but always there arose the question of whether, in a year of light snow, there ought not to have been more money left over than there was. So the various appropriations were voted: $400 for a Public Health Nurse (shared with several other towns), $25 for a cemetery caretaker, $50 for the cutting of bushes along the highways, $3200 for town poor, $750 for street lights, $1000 for repairs to schools, and $7800 for the entire school budget (which, however, is supplemented by a grant from the state and from tuition charged out-of-town pupils attending school here). One of the selectmen moved that at a certain spot the bank and sides of the road should be removed. The $150 it would cost to remove those embankments, he contended, would be saved in snow-removal costs avoided many times over. For, said he, "there's an eight-foot drift there even when there's no snow at all!"

The high school is dismissed for these Town Meetings and attends in a body, seated in bleachers on the stage of the hall. It is considered a necessary part of their education in democratic procedures. Some years there are verbal fireworks, but this year Town Meeting was placid indeed. No controversial issues were raised. We missed the usual row over whether or not to fence the cemetery. The issue was not even brought up. After many years' discussion the cemetery remains unfenced. One road question brought forth the remark "This Article ain't wrote right. It don't pass the law. I wrote it, too!" And after the sympathetic chuckle died down the speaker continued, "We can postpone the Article and we'll get the road built accordin' to law." And of course we will.

There is a remarkable sense of dignity in these meetings. The hall is sparsely furnished with benches, a few chairs, and some bleacher seats, for it is used mostly for basketball games. The men line up along the back wall, the women occupy the benches. When the latter are seated, some of the older men take what seats are left. Soon the air is blue with smoke. There is a certain murmuring of quiet conversation in the corners. After each Article of the warrant is read there is a grave and traditional silence. It may be the most routine matter, one that is always brought up and always decided a certain way, probably always will be. Even so, there is no undue haste to dispose of the matter. The Moderator reads the Article and then this silence is preserved just as if the idea were brand-new and needed serious thought, though the Town Report, with all the matters listed in it, has been out for a week and everyone has had a chance to study it and make up his mind about it. After a proper interval someone eventually breaks the silence with a "Mr. Moderator, I move you—" Again there is a discreet and decorous silence before the motion is seconded. In fact, often the Moderator has to ask, "Is the motion supported?" When an amendment is needed there is a friendly asking— across the hall—"I'll amend that, George, if it's all right with you," and the first speaker affably allows that it's all right with him. If the matters of amendment grow too complicated, the maker of the original motion withdraws his motion and so do the various amenders and seconders, and we start over again.

There is not much chance for "political corruption" when things are thus talked over and made public. Those who are behind in their taxes, those who receive town help—and there are too many of them these long hard winters—have their names and the amounts they receive all published in the Town Meeting report, and anybody is at liberty to question the legitimacy of any expenditure. One year we had an amusing time deciding the difference between fire wards and fire wardens, but somehow we carry on, and if the matters that are voted at Town Meeting are not carried out to everybody's satisfaction, there is always next year's Town Meeting coming up, when the town officers can be called to account.

And then, whether the meeting has been placid or lively, friendly or a bit acrimonious, it is all forgotten and life swings back to normal in the evening at "Town Meeting Ball," where the first selectman turns fiddler and the constable plunks a guitar and young and old dance from eight o'clock to midnight, and large quantities of soft drinks and hot dogs are consumed for the benefit of the high school gymnasium building fund. American Democracy is a wonderful thing!

Our men may be silent and deliberate about their decisions; "moderate" is the word we use up here for that particular kind of unhurried gentleness. But the most "moderate" swing into purposeful and competent action when there is an emergency. One evening in the summer word went out swiftly that a ten-year-old boy was lost. He had been playing cowboys with other children back of the old high school building, in the edge of the woods. He had a lively imagination and the play was evidently so real to him that he had pursued his "bandits" farther into the wilderness than he had ever been before, and then those thick black woods had filled up with darkness before he had realized that it was getting to be supper time. When he didn't come in at dusk the family began to worry. His mother called and blew the whistle which had always been his signal to come home. When it got to be nine o'clock and he still hadn't appeared, his father spoke to two or three of the men, who swiftly summoned others, and in no time at all a posse of searchers was organized. These men are used to stalking game, they can move quietly in the woods, and their alert eyes and ears are quick to notice even the smallest signs—the disturbances of earth or plant, heel mark or broken twig. But it was after dark, and rugged terrain.

Along with the boy's father our neighbor Dwight, one of the many guides this country has produced, led the men into a spreading fan from the point back of the school, where the boys had last seen him. Dwight knew, and one or two of the other men knew, that somewhere back in there was an old well, probably uncovered, or perhaps with a cover so weather-beaten and rotten that a boy's weight would break it through easily. But they said nothing to the father. There was no need of adding to his fear. They managed to examine the area carefully, however, and found no sign of disturbance. It was a chilly night and this lad was not strong. When no sign of him had been found by midnight, men from a nearby Army airbase were called in to help. The fear that clutched at every heart was that perhaps he had tripped over a stump or fallen over a ledge and might lie unconscious and be entirely passed by in the darkness. Calling to each other, to keep in touch, they combed those woods for a distance of a mile and a half, which led them over the crest of a hill in the thickest kind of going. If the boy had gone so far as that he would indeed be turned around and find it hard to get back to cleared land. Maine woods can be awfully dense with small growth of spruce and fir packed close—and windfalls and ledges and boggy spots. Woodland bogs in this country are to be respected. Many of them are well nigh bottomless, and unwary hunters have been trapped more than once.

The boy's mother, with a brave heart and a steady faith, kept praying, and while she prayed she kept hot coffee on the stove for the weary searchers. Her husband's mother, who made her home with them, was a wise and levelheaded woman. In fact she is our town clerk who keeps the town records and minutes of the meetings so clearly in spite of sometimes confusing debate. But on this night of endlessness even her serenity was put to excruciating test. Nobody mentioned the possibility of bears—but we all knew that there were bear in those woods and that a child might well appeal to a mother bear with hungry cubs. It was a time of year when cubs would be growing fast. There was also the remote possibility of a bull moose, the most formidable animal of our country when alarmed. And we have bobcat in this wilderness, too, though they are not likely to attack anything but young deer unless they feel themselves cornered. But quite apart from these possibilities was always the more likely and more serious one—a fall, with a broken limb, or possibly concussion, or severe bleeding. And even if the boy were not hurt, he could wander a long time without being found and the fright of night and hunger in cold thick woods could be pretty bad.

Along toward dawn, when light was beginning to make the wearying task a little more hopeful, some of the men, working ahead of the group a bit, noticed a thickening in a tree that wasn't quite the right size or shape for porcupine. And sure enough, there was the boy, uncomfortably asleep. Being a true two-gun cowboy, he had a holster belt as well as the belt that held up his trousers. And he had taken these two belts and lashed himself to the crotched trunk, his feet braced against the other side of the crotch, and leaning back against the larger trunk, he had dozed off into a light sleep. He explained to his father later that when he knew for sure he was lost he decided that that was safer than lying on the cold damp ground, and that he knew by daylight someone would come and find him! Thus are levelheaded woodsmen made.

In the center of Franklin a tiny thread of a stream wanders through alder growth near the railroad station. One day the station agent, looking out of his window, saw a big shining red car with out-of-state license plates stop beside this stream. The man who got out matched the car. He was dressed in expensive fishing togs; with new creel and fly rod he advanced toward the brook. The station agent left his post and sauntered over. He stood watching the stranger for a minute.

The fisherman spoke first. "Any trout in this brook?" His tone was patronizing.

The agent spat thoughtfully. "Might be," he answered laconically. "Or might not. Never can tell about trout. But I wouldn't fish that brook if I was you, mister."

"And why not, I'd like to know?" The stranger was truculent now.

"Well," said Mike, "people round here kinda leave that brook for the kids. I wouldn't like to say what might happen to you or that car of yours if they was to catch you fishin' here."

And without a backward look Mike sauntered off. He had the day before stocked that brook from a shipment of fingerlings from the State Hatchery that had come through his office. For years he has seen to it that there are trout there "for the kids." I don't know whether, as guardian of the brook, he also enjoys some sport there. After all—a station agent's job doesn't give him much time to go farther afield when fishing season starts.

When he got back to the station he looked out of the window. The shiny car and the stranger had gone.

It was a warm night with a glowing, full harvest moon

rising over Schoodic Mountain. I could hardly stick to my studying for watching it and the lovely light that played over forest and meadow. Even as I watched I saw a car come up the road, stop, turn in my drive. A young girl was getting out, and as she came toward me I saw it was Blanche. As she came into the living room I saw the light of joy in her face. She wanted to tell me about plans for her marriage and to settle on a date for the ceremony. And my heart was singing inside so loudly I was afraid she might hear it—this was the third daughter of the plumber who for so long had nursed the hurt over the plumbing incident. Evidently the old resentment no longer held them all in its iron grip. After Blanche told me of her plans and shared her joy with me, I asked her if her father approved of her asking me to perform the ceremony, and she said, "Oh yes, he's glad."

Her mother was in a nursing home with a slowly progressing illness of a very serious nature. I had been in to see her a few times and she had always seemed glad that I had come. Here was this girl of nineteen coming to her wedding with no chance of talking things over with her own mother. I was glad she had wanted to come to see me, and I tried to help her feel secure and joyful and reverent, in addition to the eagerness which she obviously had. She made a beautiful bride, with her copper-colored hair shining under its simple white cap with finger-length veil. Though she had two older married sisters, she had chosen her wedding dress and made her preparations pretty much by herself. The wedding was in her own home, and the father smiled at me as he gave her away into the keeping of the fine lad to whom she had given her heart. I am sure the minister at that wedding must have looked almost as radiant as the bride, I was rejoicing so deeply that somehow the old wound had healed over. And two years later, when the mother died, they asked me to conduct her funeral service, rather than having the minister of the church they were now attending. Very simply the explanation was given—"You've known her so much longer, and this was the church she always did attend. We're glad you can do it for us."

Not far from their house was a fine square gray house of beautiful proportions. Two sisters lived there who had been known all their long lives as "The Girls." One of them had been the town music teacher and the organist at the church. Practically everyone of the last generation who could play any instrument in this or the neighboring towns had come under her gentle tutelage. The young girls grew up longing to be like this teacher, with her careful speech, pretty clothes, and ladylike ways. Many are the stories of her ways of interesting her pupils. She nearly always presented her lesson with a story to loosen up the minds of her little pupils and keep them from self-consciousness, just as she had them loosen their fingers by exercising them before they started to play. And she not only gave hours of time to playing the organ at the village church here but went faithfully to Bar Harbor, where she was organist in one of the larger churches. Each summer she would hold a recital—at which delicious punch and cookies were served, prepared by the other sister, whose self-effacing ways made it possible for this one to be away from home pursuing her musical career. The house with its ample and gracious porch, set on a rise of ground well back from the highway, was a reflection of their well-ordered life.

There was a central hall with a graceful staircase, to the left a formal parlor, and behind it a music room, with a

bust of Beethoven and a metronome on the piano, so beautifully polished and cared for. The walls of this room had
pictures of musicians—Liszt, Chopin, Schubert, and the boy
Handel, discovered playing in the attic by his nightcapped
father who held a lantern high over the startled lad.

On the right of the entrance was the family sitting room,
and back of it the dining room. The furniture was beautiful
old mahogany, with graceful lines and a soft dull polish that
spoke of many years of loving care. The walls of the sitting
room were painted a delicate robin's-egg blue. This made
the background for some oil paintings and a most amusing
old print of a great many cats with wonderful expressions,
playing like children on a seesaw. I suppose it was a print
that dates back to the early days of lithography. The chief
point of interest in the room was the amazing and decorative use of twigs with birds' nests fastened to them which
were put up on the wall, making an interesting pattern of
dark forms with light spaces between. There were nests of
chimney swifts, orioles, vireos, warblers, a humming bird's
nest, and even the large gray balloon of a paper wasp's nest.
Thus they brought the outdoors into the house with such
good taste and sense of the decorative that it was not in the
least rustic or messy, but fitted in with the fine furniture,
the old brass warming pan, and the large brass kettle for
wood that stood beside the Franklin stove. There were choice
books on the marble-topped table under the mirror, and the
Boston rocker and rush-bottomed chair, and the lovely old
horsehair-covered sofa, gave a welcome to anyone who
would linger awhile in this attractive room.

They always liked to have visitors see their cat Mittie,
who could walk on her hind legs for a tidbit of fish, jump
through a hoop, and perform various other tricks. It must

have taken hours of patient teaching. Their former cat had been named for a friend whom it somehow resembled. But one day it was discovered that this cat, Caroline, was a tom, and ever afterward it was called Caroline He.

The first time I called there I found the bird's nests a fine point of departure for conversation, and presently one of the sisters, her head cocked slightly to one side and her eyes bright, almost like a bird herself, was telling me of a robin family that had built on a low limb of their apple tree, where they could watch it from the window. At one point, when the four baby birds were ravenous, Father Robin arrived with a particularly fat and long worm, and, seeing so many mouths, thought to save labor. He put one end of the worm into one open mouth and the other end into another, and there they were, each choking because he could not swallow. Father flew off, well pleased with his ingenuity, but Mother arrived in time, saw what was happening, "and," said this prim little lady, "she hopped up on the edge of the nest and with one clip of her bill cut the worm in two and went off clucking, 'Just like a man!'"

It was always a matter of amazement to these dear ladies that I was not afraid to live alone or to travel the roads at night in my car. True "gentlewomen," they had been brought up in an era when girls and women were not so independent. But I saw in them an aristocracy of thought and a careful, gentle way of life that I wish we might retain in these more slapdash days.

I never did tell them of the frosty winter night when the thermometer stood at eighteen above zero and I had walked part way home. I had been called out for an emergency and when at half past two in the morning the car refused to start I had set out to walk back the three miles to my house.

It was a beautiful night—still and cold, the pale waning moon touching the bay-ice to silver. The snow was crisp and squeaky under my feet and quiet loveliness lay upon the world. I was tired and sleepy but enjoying the walk, until about a mile and a quarter from home, I saw a car coming toward me. The men in it, seeing who I was, stopped, turned around, and said, "Can't we take you home, Mrs. Henrichsen?" and I got in gratefully. Although the car already had five big men, all smoking furiously, they made room for me and I was glad of the lift up the hill to the parsonage. But perhaps it was just as well that none of the neighbors saw whose car it was that I got out of at three in the morning!

Certainly "The Girls" would have been horrified if they had known.

FIFTEEN

SIGNS OF PROGRESS CREEP INTO THIS COUNTRY, AND SOME OF us question whether all this that is labeled progress really is. Surely we rejoice over the new high school—a fine building with well-lighted classrooms, science laboratory, shop, home economics department, a cafeteria, and a gymnasium and auditorium still in process of construction. It is a far cry from the old three-room building, so terribly overcrowded. Now there is a new spirit among the students—more aliveness, for there is more for them to do. There is more seriousness in study and less fooling. Some of us who thought that efforts to raise money for band instruments were a little premature, since the auditorium was not even completed, have been quite won over as we have seen the interest the boys and girls are taking in learning to play. They are blissfully unaware of the lessons they are learning in teamwork, in subordination of self to the harmony of the whole, the necessity for the discipline of practice; but we

who see it rejoice. Everyone holds his head higher because of the martial strains that come from the cafeteria, where band practice is held every Wednesday afternoon.

The practical training in use of tools and in general "know-how" that our boys are getting in the shop course is reflected in their general pride in increased competence. Now those who are not on the basketball team may still excel in something. In the old days those who were not athletic received little recognition. The next generation ought not to have so many families who are hard-pressed financially, for more of our men will have been trained for many trades. However, the general ability of our men to turn their hands to anything needful constantly amazes me. Maine men who are fishermen also know something about farming and practically any of them can repair a boat, raise a house and put new stringers under it, tinker an old car back into running order, build a kitchen cabinet, or install a plumbing system. When we add knowledge of power tools and trade requirements to this native "know-how" our boys should be among the most capable in America. And it is a well-known fact that manual skill usually makes for mental alertness. Education of mind and hand go together. It is proving so in our new school.

I suppose the advent of television into our country was inevitable. More and more of the houses are showing those strange antennae. I must say they seem more appropriate on apartment house roofs than they do on our little houses. To me they seem like silly man-made gestures against the eternal message of the pointed spires of balsam and spruce, and against the stars they disappear altogether. I have yet to learn that here is any real and permanent advantage to our way of life. But I know that many of our people will still prefer to watch the gulls wheeling against the scudding clouds, or a red squirrel angrily frisking his tail as he scolds a passing cat, to the faces of advertisers talking endlessly on a silver screen to induce the purchase of this brand of soap or that kind of cigarette. Like any new thing it will have its fad, but I am guessing that for most Maine men and women the endless and familiar yet ever changing pageant of birds and boats, weather and sky, sunset and moonrise, will hold the permanent satisfactions.

And while the modern school is unquestionably a great improvement to our life, and the coming television very much a question as far as I am concerned, I am reactionary enough to deplore the modernization of our stores. We used to enter buildings which were the social centers of their part of town. With lamps, rubber boots, fishing flies, tobacco, and first aid supplies nesting sociably together on the left, and groceries of all kinds attractively arranged on the right, with the meat counter and refrigerator and storeroom at the back, there was still room enough in the far corner near the stove for the men of the community to get together and settle the affairs of the hunting season, the fishing possibilities, the town politics, or the Presidential election. There was a genuineness about these "cracker-barrel sessions"— though there was no barrel, and the crackers had long since been coming in the conventional gay-colored packages—that I hate to lose. It was the place where one felt the pulse of the town, and the preacher, lingering over her purchases, could sometimes know what the non-church-going menfolk of the town were really thinking.

That day has gone. The stores have become "super-markets" complete with fluorescent lights and carriages for one's groceries. The rubber boots and first aid supplies are still there, but in a back corner department by themselves. Everything is very compact, very modern. There are no broad corners where men find it comfortable to linger. Maybe it is progress, but I wonder. I used to love to go into one of those stores, and although it was some distance from the parsonage I found it convenient to shop there frequently. Now only the fact that it has the best meat for miles around takes me in at all—and always with a feeling of homesickness for something intangible but real and solid and worthwhile that I have not yet found in the new. Perhaps the store owners are making a better profit this way. I sincerely hope so. They are fine young people with a strong influence for good in the town. And perhaps in a few more years there will be more mellowness here and less of the shiny new. At least we will all be more used to it.

One of the older men who had had a slight stroke and whose mind was sometimes a bit vague, and sometimes keener than we could guess because of his difficulty in expressing his thought, said one day: "That is the trouble with progress anyhow—it is just going on and on and on!" I am not sure what he was trying to say, but I think, from his discouraged tone and from having known the general trend of his thought, that he was trying to say that progress, just going on and on and on, isn't enough. Evolution will never save the world. There isn't any social evolution that we can trust to bring in a better order of things. There must be creative expression of the goodness of God, cutting across the accepted ways by daring souls who have a high vision, a deep commitment and a tremendous patience, and a willingness to sacrifice, if need be to die, for that which is Highest and Holiest.

One day on the way back from the store I stopped in to see Mrs. Johnson, a rare and wonderful lady, ninety years old, who has been spending the last four years writing a history of Sullivan. What an interest it has been for her! Confined to the couch and a chair, she has written, day after day, picking with two fingers at a typewriter, writing endless letters to people to get the facts of their family genealogies. She has completed a work that will prove a fine source of information for all the descendants of these early families. I hope she has included the story of the tinker who use to come through here. She remembers his visits when she was a child, his pots and kettles strapped on his back. They said he had no settled home but slept under an overturned boat on the beach. Where he spent the winters no one knew, but when spring came "Kling Klang," as they called him because of the jingling noise of the tinware, would show up, making his way over the countryside on stilts that he might cover the distance faster.

As Easter approached again I was "right out straight," as we say, when we want to express utter busyness. I love that expression—it always suggests pictures of a cocker spaniel racing before the wind, his legs stretched to their farthest, nose alert, ears streaming back "right out straight."

There were families to be seen who were ready to come into church membership or to have their babies christened —there were plans for the services—consultations with our organists about the music, bulletins to be arranged and mimeographed. In addition to the regular services we were this year to have an Easter sunrise service. It was scheduled for seven o'clock, a bit after sunrise to be sure, but the sun would not be any more than peeping over the mountain and shining back to us from the windows of Bar Harbor across the bay.

Easter morning dawned, clear and cold. The tennis court in the center of town, the only flat place overlooking the bay, was in full sunlight but there was still an inch of snow underfoot. About forty people came. We had a Chaplain's portable field organ to use and we stood there looking out across the sparkling sea to the lovely powder-blue mountains beyond—feeling the warmth of the sun as it climbed over the mountain to caress our backs. How the voices rang out on "Christ the Lord Is Risen Today." Nobody thinks of it now as a "homely hymn." Its triumphant ringing Allelulias seemed to reach out to the very top of Cadillac Mountain with the glad good news of a Lord of Life who could not be held by sin and death and who rises to make Himself known in human hearts and express Himself through human lives. The thrilling fact gave an extra shine of gladness to the eyes of the village people as they gathered for this brief half-hour service. Then the young people sped away to the vestry where the church women were preparing an Easter breakfast, while I hustled home to gather myself together before the strenuous and glorious day ahead.

What an Easter it was, crowded churches beautiful with Easter lilies, babies to be christened, older people coming so gladly into the active fellowship of the church—an attendance all told of nearly six hundred people by the time I had made the rounds of the churches. And in every face the sincerity of feeling which is so real among these "Down East" folk.

Soon after Easter I stopped in at the home of one of our

young women who has started a small florist business for herself. With a great love of flowers and a need to supplement the family income, Evon has added to her responsibilities a little greenhouse. It keeps her busy. Her two small children, Jon and Heather, are among my favorite parishioners. They are regularly at church. Heather brings her doll and sometimes both Heather and the doll go to sleep. Jon is quite grown up now, but ever since he heard a sermon—he couldn't have been more than four years old then—from the text, "There was a man sent from God whose name was John," he has felt that the church and the work of God's kingdom are especially his. He is truly "one sent from God," and he takes the offering with as much dignity and faithfulness as an older usher might.

I stopped there because I wanted to place an order for some pansy plants. Evon is making pansies something of a specialty and has a number of choice varieties which she has grown from seed. The rich earth and the cool winds off the sea seem especially favorable for her pansies, as well as for the roses, delphinium, stock, and other lovely things that fill her yard all summer long. She has the most beautiful madonna and regal lilies I think I ever saw. All this, in addition to a growing family, some kittens, a litter of beautiful cocker spaniel pups, she still finds time to give love and devotion to her church, and not only supplies pulpit flowers but with her family is in her pew at nine-thirty every Sunday morning.

The family of the Superintendent of Schools are also staunch supporters of the church. When this fine young father with his lovely wife and four eager and sometimes irrepressible children are there together, as they usually are, it gives the day something very special for the pastor. Sturgis, a responsible lad of twelve, Stephanie, ten, Heidi, the shy one whose valentine I treasure, and little Jeffrey, who finds it hard to remain decorous in church for an hour, are the sort of children who will carry forward the same kind of fineness of spirit and character that we have seen and loved in the older generation. When one visits that home it is easy to see where the alertness in their faces comes from. It is a home where children's interests are encouraged and their treasures valued. Pictures of dogs, or birds, baseball players, or whatever is the hobby of the moment, are cut from magazines, mounted on gay construction paper, and hung in the den. There are books everywhere. Each child has his family responsibilities and chores, each child's personal property is respected, and the eager minds are encouraged to grow, to ask questions and to find answers. It is for them and for Heather and Jon in Sorrento, as well as for little Charles and Jean and the three bright-eyed Preble children, and all the other loyal children in each of the churches, that I struggle to have a children's sermon each week. It is good discipline for me, for when I have the main point of the sermon clear-cut enough and simply stated so that I can put it in story form for the children, then I can know it is clear enough in my mind to be spoken with conviction in the main sermon. I think I would rather be a good pastor to these children than anything else on earth—and I pray that I may not disappoint their faith, or by any lack of sensitiveness to them make them think less of the love God has for them, nor of the importance of His church in their lives.

One of the calls I most enjoy making is on Captain Miller, a fine old gentleman of ninety-six whose seafaring life, when he was Captain on the Ward line, holds many interesting tales. He likes to tell how as a boy he ran away from home, shipped on a passing vessel, and was later wrecked and driven ashore near here. There is no doubt about his sense of dignity as Captain, nor of his assurance in handling ship and men in time of storm or other crisis. His eyes, keen and penetrating, are still in good order and he reads without glasses everything except the finest print. Now he boards in Prospect Harbor within sight and smell of the sea.

Fishermen are, as a rule, not overtalkative. One of them said to me once, speaking of an enthusiastic lady of our acquaintance: "She's a fine woman. Only trouble is she talks faster than anyone can listen." Another summed up a certain speech he had heard: "He talked more than he had things to say." When they do have something to say it is direct and to the point.

An artist friend of mine was painting along this shore. He has a great gift for catching the light as it plays on the weather-beaten fish houses, the shine of wet rocks, the glitter of sun on water, the bright haze of fog. I think he gets more "weather" into his pictures than anyone whose work I have ever seen. The realism of that weather was attested to one day when a fisherman, passing him as he went down across the beach to his dory, stopped to watch him work. For a long time he said nothing, but then, in the gentle voice that all these men have, he said: "Now do you care if I say somethin' that ain't real nice about that picture?"

And the artist replied, "No, I wish you would."

With great earnestness the fisherman continued: "Now that cloud up in the corner ain't goin' to do you no good. I've sot my net time and time again when them scuds was shootin' up over Schoodic head, and they ain't no fish to be had. You might as well haul up and go home. I say get that cloud outa there."

The Woman's Society of this church meets regularly every week to make aprons and braided rugs, to make patchwork quilts and embroidered and crocheted articles for the fair which is held every summer. It is at these work sessions that I catch the pulse of their thinking, and always I come back humbled by their devotion, grateful for their common sense. With great good nature, matters affecting the church life and work are talked over, plans made for future events. They send cards or "sunshine baskets" to the sick and shut-ins, and out of the community of work and thought comes community of feeling and a sense of solidarity.

One day when I "happened in" they were looking at an old quilt top that someone had given them—a fascinating pattern of early patchwork print—mostly brown materials with fine small figures. The white squares of unbleached muslin between the printed pieces were stained and sun-burned and the women were talking about using what they could of it but adding bright new materials to make it more colorful. "Oh don't," I exclaimed. "There aren't too many of these old prints left. If you'll fix it up with a new backing I'll gladly buy it at the fair next summer. You can mark it for me."

They looked at me as if I were crazy. To think that any-one would prefer the dull old prints to the bright new gay ones that could be had so easily. But good-naturedly they agreed to put new muslin squares in place of the stained ones and a new backing and put it in good shape. I'm sure there was general perplexity over my idea of what was pretty.

When Christmas came there was a large package all done up in gay paper under the pulpit and when I opened the card I found that these dear ladies were making me a present

of the quilt—so much more work for them than it would
have been to make it all of new material, for all the old
pieces had been carefully ripped out and set between new
pieces of white. When I tried to thank them one of them
said, with a wag of her head which spoke volumes, "Well,
we thought that if you wanted anything like that you ought
to have it!"

And presently it was June again and time for graduation.
The high school young people had brought cedar boughs
from the woods and the old town hall was transformed. How
good it smelled! By covering the entire front wall, and the
sides of the room, and the back of the stage with chicken
wire and then putting sprays of cedar packed close into that
wire, they had made a really beautiful setting for their
graduation exercises. The class numerals, cut out of white
paper, were fastened against the green over the stage. It had
taken the better part of the week to get things ready. Each
day the boys had gone out to the woods and cut the truck
loads of cedar and brought them back to the hall, where
with the girls they had all worked together on this deco-
rating, while in and through the working group the school
chorus rehearsed their graduation songs, and the frightened
valedictorian practiced her address.

Graduation night came, hot and breathless. The room was
packed with families, relatives, and friends. Presently the
music teacher, slightly excited and wearing a corsage of red
roses on her black evening dress, took her place at the piano
and began the processional. The class marshals in cap and
gown led the procession, the juniors, in evening dress, first,
followed by the rest of the school. On each side of the
center aisle they stood while the marshals went back to the

door to lead the seniors, the boys in green caps and gowns with white tassels on the caps, the girls in white caps and gowns with green tassels. In the audience little brothers and sisters craned their necks or stood on their chairs to see, mothers whispered excitedly, "There he comes now," fathers, hot and uncomfortable in their best suits, were certain that no girls anywhere were as pretty as their own daughters. It was just as it should be—simple, beautiful, a bit emotional. As I stood looking into the faces of the townspeople on the floor below me and at the lovely serious young faces of the graduates on the stage, I could hardly steady my voice to give the invocation properly. These were my people, my friends. They had trusted me with their worries and their joys. Many of them who never came to church still felt free to "call on" as we say, when there was trouble of any sort. I had been in most of these homes, eaten at many a kitchen table with them, baptized their babies, buried their dead. I was part and parcel of their lives, and they of mine. How much they had given to me in these years. The friendships may have seemed slow in forming—but formed they were forever.

At the close of the ceremonies, after the Superintendent of Schools had taken the diplomas from the hand of the principal and given them to the graduates, shaking hands with each one, who then, as he turned from the desk proudly moved the tassel on his cap from the left to the right, the audience rose as the chorus sang the school Alma Mater. As I moved to the front of the stage to give the benediction I saw in these boys and girls the finest hope of our nation—young people, clear-eyed, joyful, fine in their ideals and purposes, carrying a heritage of Maine strength and common sense and simplicity. Instead of the words I had planned to use there came to mind a benediction I had heard once and had used occasionally for weddings. I used it now.

May the grace of God be in your eyes, to minister to His joy,
May the grace of God be on your lips, to minister to His truth,
May the grace of God be in your hands, to minister to His helpfulness,
May the grace of God be in your hearts, that all men may know the Love of God through Jesus Christ our Lord.

Down at the end of the point, where Winter Harbor on one side and Prospect Harbor on the other have given haven to lobster boats, lies a large part of Acadia National Park, and at the very end of it is Schoodic Head. It is the place where we take our visitors first. It is the great rocky promontory where we all go after a storm to see the surf. Farther out to sea than any part of Mount Desert Island, it is perhaps as beautiful a spot as any on this rugged forested coast. It is the place where one can go for a lobster picnic, or for quiet meditation and inspiration. I went down there the day after graduation, in the late afternoon.

The sun was beginning to drop low behind Cadillac, throwing the mountain into deep purple shadow and making a golden glory above and behind it that was reflected in the water. Close to the rocks where I stood, tasting the salt spray, the long green swells rose and fell. What mighty power lay under those lifting waves. Clear, translucent, green they rose and curled to crash into white foam—but out to sea all was a quiet gray. A cormorant flew low along the edge of the rocks—herring gulls lifted and wheeled and

settled again just below me, where the stunted balsams and
lichen-covered rocks met the rosy granite. Then suddenly
I saw a great bird coming—big as a goose—white. Then I
saw the wing tips, as black as if they had been dipped
in India ink, and ruled straight across at the elbow, too.
Gannets! We don't often see them so close in shore, but a
pair flew by that night. The sun was gone now and dusk
was closing in over the water. A great blue heron, trailing
his long legs, flew across, going from the frog-filled marshes
behind me to the tall trees up on the headland where his
nest was. And down below, serene and confident on that
tumbling water, a little duck was riding—a bufflehead, so
tiny, so unafraid. Surely the spirit of God still moves upon
the face of the deep.

I turned away to drive back home across this dear Maine
land, passing one after another of the tiny buildings where
we worship together, perfectly certain of one thing—that no
matter how few in numbers the congregations I was called
to serve, there are no little churches in the Kingdom of God.
There is no such thing as a small church when it is a church
of Jesus Christ.